Ray Charles
raymondcharlesiii@yahoo.com

Color Struck(America's racial profile in legal documents).

By Ray Charles
Word count: 46,881

Foreword

When Mississippi seceded from the union, it issued a Declaration of the Immediate Cause which Induces and Justify the Secession of the State of Mississippi from the Federal union.

Specifically:

> *"In the momentous step which our State [Mississippi] has taken of dissolving its connection with the government of which we so long formed a part, **it is but just that we should declare the prominent reasons which have induced our course.***
>
> *Our position is thoroughly identified with the institution of slavery–the greatest material interest of the world. Its labor supplies the product which constitutes by far the largest and most important portions of commerce of the earth. These products are peculiar to the climate verging on the tropical regions, and by an imperious law of nature, none but the black race can bear exposure to the tropical sun. These products have become necessities of the world, and a blow at slavery is a blow at commerce and civilization. That blow has been long aimed at the institution, and was at the point of reaching its consummation. There was no choice left us but submission to the mandates of abolition, or dissolution of the Union, whose principles had been subverted to work out our ruin."*

A declaration by Confederate States Vice-President Alexander H. Stephens, On March 21, 1861:

> *"But not to be tedious in enumerating the numerous changes for the better, allow me to allude to one other though last, not least. The new constitution has put at rest, forever, all the agitating questions relating to our peculiar institution African slavery as it exists amongst*

> us the proper status of the Negro in our form of civilization."

The conclusion is clear; the civil war was caused by the determination of the State of Mississippi and other Southern States, to protect the institution of slavery.

Accepting this reality, along with other historical events, the lives of our ancestors are drawn into focus. Examining their religious beliefs and social ideas has opened my mind to a clearer view of the days of their lives.

To accomplish this, I don't force them into my present, I travel back to their time, and by doing this their ancient world becomes familiar, anchored in real places with their lives open before me like a book. I then realize that my ancestral characters loved and hated, succeeded and failed, laughed and cried--just like we do today. I am puzzled though, why such human traits were not ascribed to all men, as lamented by the dramatic testimony and acts by Mississippians that showed not all Mississippians embraced slavery to such destructive measures as their fellow citizens. Consider the following petitions by Mississippians and feel the gist of my story:

***

Petition: 11082002
State: Mississippi
Year: 1820
Abstract: Slave owner William Johnson, having previously freed a female slave named Amey in Louisiana, now seeks to free Amey's son, William. Johnson asks the legislature for permission "to make that disposition of his property most agreeable to his feelings & consonant to humanity." He adds that emancipation will "give that Liberty to a human being which all are entitled to as a Birthright, & extend the hand of humanity to a rational creature, on whom unfortunately Complexion, Custom & even Law in this Land of Freedom,

has conspired to rivet the fetters of Slavery." **Results are unknown**.

***

Petition: 11082101
State: Mississippi
Year: 1821
Abstract: About 1818, John Morin purchased his eighteen-month-old slave daughter, described as a "quartroon" girl named Adele. Morin then went to the justice of the peace in Hancock County and procured an "act of emancipation." A short time later Morin died. His mother, Louise Favre, discovered that the act was not valid. She asks the legislature for an act of emancipation to free Adele. Favre states that she has six children by her former husband, Peter Morin, and that one of them is threatening to keep Adele in bondage. The mother laments that she is growing old and wants to respect her son's wish before she dies." **Petition granted**.

***

Petition: 11083007
State: Mississippi
Year: 1830
Abstract: Eleven Jefferson County residents ask for the emancipation of Elizabeth, a sixty- or seventy-year-old slave. Elizabeth's owner, Isaac Corey, said on his death bed that he wished her to be freed and that after his debts were paid the residue of his estate should be paid to her. The citizens seek to carry out Corey's final wish. "What language can speak," the petitioners explain, "or logic point out more Cogent reasons for the liberation of a human being born, by Nature to enjoy the Vital air as free as it blows, what bosom Can feel an unfriendly sentiment to the unchaining of but a morsel of an Old age in bondage—Nature in a few years more will Claim & take her Own." **Petition granted**.

***

COMMENT: *This petition touched my heart and it is such a pity that Isaac Corey did not realize the value of freedom for Elizabeth's life until his own life was at an end…Nevertheless; he came to realize that life and freedom were sacred and he had friends who were able to act on his behalf for Elizabeth's sake.*

The courageous acts by the Eleven Jefferson County residents shows that in the antebellum South customs and courtesies were sometimes placed at the borders of interracial reality and often an intangible truth emerged, signifying that there are stories hidden deep in the archives of historical obscurity. Stories that are seldom present or told in the popular mainstream histories of the antebellum south and when acknowledged they are only hinted at with a flavor of recognition. Yet beneath its structure it is sometimes the back-story of great American classics and therein lays a mystery or perhaps, more of an aberrant narrative that intertwines with so many lives of Southern Black and White Americans that it is often difficult to plot their separate interests. Their laughter, their voices and their cries we will never hear, but a hint of their echoes have been preserved in these legal petitions. Therefore no grammar or spelling corrections have been made in respect to the petition…as they were recorded, so they are presented to you.

Introduction

The idea for writing this book came to me during my genealogy research, which has revealed to me a truth that had been on the edges of my consciousness since childhood; first, as an unverified oral tradition and now as a sourced testament to the identity of my ancestors.

I once believed that my ancestral identity was one of "descendant of Slaves and Native Americans." Now I know that I am a descendant of Slaves; Slave Holder and Indian alike and forced to analyze slavery and its effect on my ancestors and their relationships to one another and not just as an embarrassing moment in American History.

It is amazing how close some of our ancestral heroes were in their opinions about slavery even as they opposed each other on the battle field:

> *"There are few, I believe, in this enlightened age, who will not acknowledge that   slavery as an institution is a moral and political evil".* – Gen. Robert E. Lee.

In agreement, Lee's contemporary, Abraham Lincoln attributed the incalculable   suffering experienced by our Nation during the Civil War as God's punishment on a Nation that had tolerated slavery.

The purpose of my genealogy research is to provide my family, nuclear and extended with original sourced materials on the lives of our ancestors from our Great grandparents backwards in time for as many generations I can verify for free and enslaved ancestors. For some topics I will attempt to edit, distill, or interpret for clear and concise understanding. In all cases I will present the historical resources, for examination.

As descendants of Slaves and Slave Holders we may sometimes feel proud, angry, or ashamed of the lives our ancestors lived. From the ashes of these powerful emotions emerge many activists who are eager to tell us how we should think as a slave descendant, even going so far as to suggest that if we do not think a certain way, we have betrayed our heritage. Some have even suggested that we should demand repatriation for slavery. Have they considered that the very notion of repatriation, "AGAIN" places a price on the head of our ancestors?

All who came to America during the growing pains era contributed something to making this country the greatest on earth...our African ancestors were the first to forfeit their lives; lively hood and identities in an endeavor called indenture ship that evolved into slavery and became America's "Black Gold."

Armed with the truths I've uncovered, I can no longer rant about the evils of slavery in America without pointing a finger at our Black African ancestral kith and kin that were complicit in the slavery trade. I cannot have an unforgiving attitude towards my white ancestors, knowing that some of my black ancestors were slave owners too, and history   reminds me of the hundreds of thousands of white men who shed their blood to gain freedom for our enslaved ancestors, and thereby also freeing their White southern brothers from the chains of slaver profits.

If I glorify in the Southern Bravery and Chivalry of my white ancestor, some of whom went forth from the Southern Comfort of sprawling acres of fertile fields; antebellum plantations and homesteads to defend their way of life...I am reminded that all that is good about our southern culture was built on the institution of enslavement.

"Bread wrung from the sweat of other men's faces as wealth piled by the bond-man's two hundred and fifty years of unrequited toil."- Abraham Lincoln's   second Inaugural Address.

Slavery in America ushered in the worst type of social engineering errors of American history; and no lapse of time, or succession of generations, can purge our ancestors of the guilt of one of its first failed institutions as a free nation; that neither patriotism nor the higher obligations of Christianity can reconcile racial differences as long as we attempt to blunt the two-edged sword of historical truths, such as the misleading vague notion that " States' Rights" aside from "slavery", was the direct cause of the civil war that purged it from our society. If the two cannot be separated, then they are wrapped in one cause. Slavery!

"If only we are faithful to our past, we shall not have to fear our future. The causes of peace, justice and liberty need not fail and must not fail!"- John Foster Dulles.

Genealogy is a powerful tool that describes our ancestral relationships throughout history, but Genealogy can also be equally impressive as works of literature. It is after all, a collection of oral histories; written family traditions; photographs; official records and dossiers. Indeed, ancestral literature encompasses many authors, writing styles and subjects that have been passed down from generation to generation over hundreds of years! This ancestral literature has preserved their beliefs, values, and customs through their words and images. If nothing more, this remarkable thing that we call "genealogy" is among other things a history book, and to gain a more than casual understanding of our ancestors, we need a clear picture of the historical events that shaped their lives. From beginning to end I try to highlight the important and interesting moments that depict the creative and active hand of God at work in their lives.

During my examination of historical court and legislative records I was compelled to re-examine my beliefs and notions about America's inter-racial past. After examining historical records, one section in particular, that document Early America's appetite for interracial relationships, the behavior of our ancestors remain a mystery that is eventually understood, but cannot be explained easily. For example, prohibitions of interracial relationships, social and sexual were socially engineered to prevent the races from cohabitating and complimenting each other in marriage and other social adventures…yet it flourished! Privately and sometimes openly, the color line was crossed by all who were subject to it: Red; yellow; Black; White; Slave and Free!

Time constraints do not allow me to comment on all of the cases presented, so I simply present the information for you to analyze and form your own opinions. So much data is available until I only present those particular cases that convey the range of data that supports my thesis, that interracial relationships were inevitable as the racial populations grew. As a precautious the new country America, attempted to, but could not legislate itself out of the "melting pot" that produced complimentary traits that further fueled interracial relationships. Drawing on a wide range of legislative sources, I hope to demonstrate, in my view, had it not been for state-sponsored racism the races would have coexisted competitively and peacefully.

Although some of these cases are humorous at first glance, noting is humorous about families being torn apart white or black or the mental and physical abuse Black and White women were subjected to during domestic disputes with White and Black husbands. What I find humorous is the writing styles of some of the petitioners as they convey their anguish; grief and disgust to the public without offending the social sensitivities of that day. They accuse their partners of:

"Ungovernable temper",

"Immoral & indecent turn of mind",

"Abandoned without just cause,"

"Provocation and oppressed with a burden which none but a sufferer can feel."

And my favorite,

"Crimes, repugnant to the intentions of the marriage institution-derogatory to the dignity of her sex."

Ray Charles

Contents

Adultery & Divorce

***

Petition 11280515
North Carolina, Rowan County
December 3, 1805
Salutation: Gentlemen of the Senate & of the House of Representatives.
Abstract: Christian Limbaugh seeks a divorce from his wife, the former Catharina Hess. He asserts that Catharina, whom he left in 1799, had an "ungovernable temper" and her "immoral & indecent turn of mind led her to be connected with other men." Citing his short marriage as "a state of the most poignant misery," Limbaugh reveals that his wife was later "delivered of one or more mulatto children." He further avers that, in 1804, "at March term of the Salisbury Supr court, the said Catharina was convicted of having barbarously murdered her infant child, which was generally believed in the neighbourhood to have been a mulatto"; the governor, however, pardoned her as she stood "under the gallows." Limbaugh therefore "submits his unhappy situation to be acted upon as you in your wisdom may think fit, firmly believing that a bill of divorce will be passed in his favour."

Result: rejected.

***

Petition 11281005
North Carolina, Edgecombe County
November 20, 1810
Abstract: Isaac Bracewell states that he married Nancy Low "some years ago" and that he enjoyed "that happiness and content, which he had anticipated." He reveals, however, that the said Nancy abandoned him "without just cause, or provocation" about 1803 and that she "has ever since lived,

and continues to live in open and notorious Adultery, extending her favors, if such they can be called, to all, without distinction of color." The petitioner therefore prays that an act be passed "whereby he may be separated from the said Nancy."

Result: rejected.

***

Petition 11281010
North Carolina, Wake County
December 11, 1810
Abstract: Young Utley seeks a divorce from his wife Mary Woodward Utley, whom he married "about three years ago." Utley reveals that "some time after intermarriage the said Mary was delivered of a black child." He further reports that she is currently living in Tennessee where "she cohabits with a man of Colour, (the supposed author of her shame) in the character of a wife." At twenty-five, Utley considers himself to have "sustained an upright character" but he "is now oppressed with a burthen which none but a sufferer can feel." The petitioner therefore prays that "your Honorable body will pass a law divorcing him from his said wife."
Result: House, Senate: read, referred.

***

Petition 11281303
North Carolina, Gates County
December 13, 1813
Abstract: James Hoffler admits that his "Situation in Life is disagreeable." He reveals that he married his wife Deborah Duttons in September 1802 and that three months later she "deserted my bed and board without Cause on the part of your petitioner." Hoffler reports that his wife give birth to a child while at her father's house and then she "did take up with a man by the name of John Lowance, a person of Collow, by whom she the said Deborah had a child"; Lowance left her and Deborah moved to Charleston, South

Carolina. He further discloses that the legislature favored him a few years ago "by passing a Law divesting her the Said Deborah of all right of Dower in my property." Hoffler now prays that a law be passed "Divorcing him ... from the said Deborah."

Result: rejected.

***

Petition 11281304
North Carolina, Wake County
December 13, 1813
Abstract: Joseph Hancock seeks a divorce from his wife, the former Tabitha Askew. Hancock confides that "he is utterly at a loss in attempting to enumerate the Base Crimes which the said Tabitha has perpetuated ... crimes repugnant to the intentions of the marriage institution -- derogatory to the dignity of her sex." He discloses that the said Tabitha has "Abandoned herself to the most vile prostitution and debauchery" and has given birth to children "of various colours and complexions and nearly effected the ruin of your petitioner!" Hancock therefore prays that "his marriage with the said Tabitha may be entirely abrogated."

Result: rejected.

***

Petition 11281705
North Carolina, Bertie County
November 22, 1817
Abstract: Mary Hassell laments that her husband Benjamin "has betaken to himself as a wife & companion a negro woman, the slave & lawful property of your petitioner." Hassell admits that she has removed herself from her husband, "who is looked upon as disgraceful ... by every upright & virtuous member of civil society," in order "to relieve herself from the odious embraces of a man so entirely destitute of all the finer feelings of sensibilities." Seeking to secure to herself "the remnant of property yet remaining" and to protect any future acquisitions "from the

cruel & rapacious grasp of the monster," the petitioner implores the legislature to pass an act protecting the property still "in her possession, & all that she may ever hereafter acquire, either by her own industry or inheritance." **Result:** granted.

***

Petition 11282402
North Carolina, Washington County
November 17, 1824
Abstract: John D. Barber discloses that, after three years of marriage, his wife Mary "left his house without cause and entered into the most abandoned scenes of prostitution with black and white." Barber further reveals that said Mary "has contracted a long time since a most hateful disease" and that "she is a most uncommon drunkard and thief." The petitioner therefore prays "that the Legislature will pass a law to dissolve the bonds of matrimony between him and the said Mary Barber." Attached affidavits charge that the said Mary "is considered to be and looked upon as one of the basest prostitutes in the human family" and that she is "entirely unfit for civilized Society."

Result: No recorded result.

***

Petition 11282403
North Carolina, Wake County
November 27, 1824
Abstract: Lewis Tombereau, a native of France, laments that he married a young woman named Nancy Jolly, "to whom he was determined to stick as close as wax." Tombereau confesses, however, that by his said marriage "he linked his fortune with and intrusted his happiness to one of the most frail, lewd, and depraved, daughters of Eve." The petitioner charges that said Nancy "forsoke both his board, and bed, to cohabit with a certain mulatto Barber named Roland Colanche." Tombereau, "with the most pungent and

heart felt sorrow," reports that Nancy "has had a coloured child, and became, and continues to be, a public and notorious prostitute in the most unlimited sense of that word. She indulging in an unreserved, and promiscuous intercourse with men of every colour, age, class, and description she meets, sufficiently dissolute, licentious, and sensual, to gratify their passion, and her lust, and desire of variety." The petitioner therefore prays that he be released "from the unhallowed bonds he in an evil hour entered into."

Result: No recorded result.

Repository: North Carolina Department of Archives and History, Raleigh, North Carolina. General Assembly, Session Records, Divorce Petitions Box: 2

***

Repository: Tennessee State Library and Archives, Nashville, Tennessee.
Petition 11482106
Tennessee, Williamson County
October 9, 1821
Abstract: Catharine Smith asks for a divorce from her husband, John P. Smith, a man of "the most abandoned dissolute & dissipated description." Smith accuses her husband of "engaging in the most extravagant scenes of lewdness, drunkenness and debauchery" and confides that he "has often treated your Petitioner in an inhuman and intolerable manner by inflicting violence on her person, and that in direct violation of his matrimonial vow, he has been repeatedly engaged in illegal intimacies with the slaves there were subject to his controll." The petitioner therefore prays that "she may be divorced from her husband and that the bonds of matrimony may be entirely dissolved."

Result: committee on divorces: "Reasonable."

***

Petition 11482108
Tennessee, Grainger County
1821
Abstract: Kimble E. Midkiff confesses that he was induced by a certain older woman named Nancy "to abscond from his fathers house in company with her" and, "by her insinuating and seductive arts," she exerted an "influence over him which she had acquired by artifice & intrigue" and the two were married. Admitting that he was at the time "under the age of sixteen years" and "under the influence of the impulse of passion rather than the dictates of reason," Midkiff recounts that "he cohabited about six months with said Nancy, during all which time he conducted himself towards her as an affectionate husband and observed his matrimonial vow with the utmost fidelity." The petitioner charges that Nancy, however, "was detected in bed with a man of colour in the neighbourhood."

Result: propositions and grievances.

***

Petition 11482109
Tennessee
September 8, 1821
Abstract: Confessing that her husband David's "treatment became so intolarable that I Could not Stay with him any longer," Mary Logue seeks a divorce. She discloses that "he not only abused my person very frequently by pulling my hair and Draging me about the house by it but [threatened] to take my Life and would go to bed with Negro women." Mary, believing it not safe to stay with him, abandoned "his house and went to my Fathers whare I have Resided Ever Since and Since I have left my husbond ... still Continued in his wickedness as bad as ever." The petitioner therefore prays that she be granted a divorce.

Result: No recorded result.

***

Petition 11482202
Tennessee, Montgomery County
July 16, 1822

Abstract: William McClure accuses his wife, Rebecca Smith McClure, of cohabiting and having "sexual & carnal intercourse with a certain negro fellow Slave by name of Taff formerly the slave of your petitioner." McClure discloses that "for six months last past the said Rebecca has been Indulging at all times of the absence of her husband from home with the said negro slave, that she took him to your petitioners house and did so openly." Stating that his wife "has gone to the state of Illinois, hoping her said paramour may abscond & there indulge her wicked & debased desires," the petitioner prays that he be granted a divorce.

Result: No recorded result.

***

Petition 11482912
Tennessee, Maury County
1829

Abstract: John Rich of Maury County seeks a divorce from Susanah Moore Rich on the grounds that she "was delivered of a mulatto child" four months after their marriage. Revealing that he cannot pay "the charge of a lawyer and the fees of court ... without injury to himself," Rich therefore "prays your Honorable boddy to pass a law divorcing him from the said Susanah."

Result: No recorded result.

***

Petition 11484502
Tennessee, Anderson County
December 19, 1845 -16 January 1846

Abstract: Mary Hookins asks for a divorce from her husband William. Hookins confides that said William "was always scolding and faultfinding and frequently disturbed your petitioner's hours of repose and sleep by his certain lectures -- abusing her for merest trifles and not seeming to be satisfied, he soon resorted to whipping her." She further admits that when she "would tell him to quit mistreating her so, he said by the common law a man had a right to whip his wife, and that so long as he was a freeman he would have the right of one, and that he would whip her every day of her life if he wanted to." Mary reveals that her husband has abandoned her "and her babies to this fate and the last rumor She heard of him he had taken up with a mulatto woman and was the father of two children by her." She therefore prays that "now if your Honorable body ... will only set aside, and undue this unfortunate act of your petitioner's youthful folly, and indiscretion; she hopes she will be able to do better in a second marriage than she did in her first; for she knows she could do worse that she did when she [and] Billy Hookins became man and wife."

Result: rejected.

Repository: Tennessee State Library and Archives, Nashville, Tennessee.

***

Petition 11680602
Virginia, Prince William County
December 9, 1806
Abstract: Seventy-one residents of Prince William County testify that they are well acquainted with Daniel Rose, who married Henrietta White, also considered at the time of the marriage as a person of "good character," in February 1806. In September of the same year, however, some seven months after celebration of the wedding, Henrietta was delivered of "a mulatto child," who is thought to have been fathered by a slave belonging to her grandfather.

Furthermore, the petitioners inform the court, it is believed that Henrietta has had "criminal connection with the said negro man" since her marriage to Rose. The petitioners apply to the legislature on Daniel Rose's behalf, asking that he be released from his "unfortunate connection." **Result:** reasonable.

***

Petition 11680806
Virginia, Loudon County
December 21, 1808
Abstract: Married in 1802, Isaac Fouch lived with his wife Elizabeth for several years "in the strictest Love, Friendship and happiness." Then he discovered she possessed a "Lewd, incontinent, profligate disposition." However, "being so much attached to her person, having from his first acquaintance with her cherished the most ardent, tender affectionate Love and Regard for her and hoping that she might yet be reclaimed, treated her with all that tenderness and respect which the most upright and Virtuous Women ought to expect, admonishing her repeatedly of the Wickedness of such a course, of the Infamy and disgrace which must result from it." But his love and admonitions were to no avail and in fact had the contrary effect; he "detected her and the partner of her crimes (a certain James Watt, a man of color) in bed together." He then resolved to leave her and set out for the Western Country. He is now convinced that reconciliation can never take place, and therefore seeks a divorce.

Result: reasonable.

***

Petition 11680906
Virginia, Amherst County
December 6, 1809

Abstract: William Howard informs the court that in January 1806 he was married to Elizabeth Dean, "whose character and conduct in life, was represented" in the "most favourable point of View." He therefore "entered into the matrimonial compact with the said Elizabeth in full hopes and confidence that" she would attend to "her Bed and Board, and in all respect discharge" the duties of "a good and faithfull wife." For his part, he also determined to "perform the duties of a good and faithfull Husband." However, within a year Howard discovered that his wife was engaged in "brutal and licentious connections" with a variety of men. Still "not willing to lend too favourable an Ear to the Reports prevalant in the neighbourhood," he determined to see for himself. So it is with certainty that he can now state that upon his return home "at a late Houre," he found his wife undressed and in bed with a "Certain Aldredge Evans a Man of coulour, and reputed to be a mulatoe." Howard ordered his wife out and they have been separated ever since. Howard seeks a divorce.

Result: reasonable.

***

Petition 11681530
Virginia, Powhatan County
December 6-15, 1815

Abstract: Hezekiah Mosby asks that he be granted a divorce from his wife Betsy. He confides that he "has had cause often to suspect that she was not only, not faithful to the marriage bed, but moreover, that she bestowed her favours on men of a different colour from herself." Mosby recounts that "when his wife was about to be delivered of a child he sent for several highly respectable ladies of the neighbourhood that they might see & judge when the child was brought into the world, before any accident could happen to it." He states that they have given "affidavits to the fact of the childs being one of colour." The petitioner therefore prays "that he may be divorced from his wife Betsy aforesaid, and, (as far as any earthly Tribunal can effect it) restored to that condition which he occupied before marriage."

Result: bill drawn.

Comments: *Analyzing the details of this petition, it seems as if Hezekiah knew the habits and nature of his wife Betsy. He knew the child she was about to give birth to was probably not his child. Further, he surmised that the child would be of mixed race. Rather than place the child's life in danger by revealing his suspicions to Betsy, whereby she might abort the child, he arranged for respectable mid-wives to be present for the birth to insure the safety of the child. His actions I would say proved that he loved her enough to not let her commit murder in order to cover her wrong.*

***

Petition 11681603
Virginia, Campbell County
November 16, 1816
Abstract: In 1806, with a license from the Clerk of Court in Campbell County, free black Robert Wright married Mary Godsey, a free white woman. They were married before a "regularly Licensed Minister of the Gospel." In January 1815, Mary eloped with a white man, William Arthur, carrying "a negro Girl and other property belonging to your petitioner." Wright overtook the two in Liberty, and persuaded his wife to return, but in November 1815, the two eloped again, this time fleeing to Nashville, Tennessee. Although he knew there was a law against interracial marriage, Wright asserts that his marriage was "valid and binding." As a result, he seeks a divorce.

Result: rejected.

***

Petition 11682308
Virginia, Louisa County
December 3-6, 1823

Abstract: About 1811, Lewis Bourne married Doratha Woodall, who then enjoyed "a good and respectable character." After about five years of marriage, however, Doratha began to live in open adultery with a black man, the slave of a neighbor. She bore him two mulatto children, one of whom is still living and the unquestionable proof of her adultery. Doratha and her lover continue to live together. Lewis Bourne, her husband, claims that he has never treated his wife badly; indeed, he permitted her to live in a house on his land. He seeks a divorce.

Result: bill drawn.

***

Petition 11682408
Virginia, King William County
December 2, 1824

Abstract: Evelina Gregory Roane, "a Daughter of affluence," seeks a divorce and custody of her infant son. Evelina represents that her marriage to Newman B. Roane has been wrought with "hardship and cruelty." She confides that "she was quickly reduced to the situation of a Slave who for some unpardonable offense, was constantly under the frowns of its master." Evelina further discloses that the said Newman admitted that "he had two mulatto children then at his Brothers who were much more comely and hansome than any she would ever bear" and shortly thereafter "this negroe woman and two mulatto children were brought upon the plantation." She confesses that "her husband adopted this woman as the more eligible companion & wife," and she reveals that her husband boasted that "if he had not expected a fortune he would never have married her." Having endured and survived multiple violent assaults, she asserts that she "obtained the restraining power of the civil magistrate" to force her husband "to keep the peace toward your Petitioner for the space of twelve months." She therefore prays that "a law may pass this honorable Body Divorcing your Petitioner from her husband ... and provide in the said act of Divorce that your Petitioner may be allowed to keep the said Junius B Roane in her possession until he comes to an age proper for being put to school."

Result: reasonable.

***

Petition 11682601
Virginia, Nansemond County
December 15, 1825-8 December 1826
Abstract: David Parker represents to the legislature that in 1807 he married Jane Carter, with whom he enjoyed ten year of "uninterrupted connubial pleasure and happiness." The couple had six children. Four years after Jane Carter's death, Parker married a second time, taking as his wife one Jane Miller. Parker's second marriage, however, has not been a happy one. He charges that his wife of four years has been guilty of "the greatest luridness, immorality and vice." She has frequently engaged in "criminal intercourse with slaves or persons of color." She also has given birth to "one or more children of color" before abandoning him and moving to North Carolina. Parker seeks a divorce. **Result:** bill drawn.

***

Petition 11683312
Virginia, James City County
December 10, 1833
Abstract: In 1821, Joseph Gresham married Sarah W. Christian of Charles City County. The couple lived in "harmony, confidence, and affection," until Gresham discovered that his wife was having an affair. Gresham notes that the charge of adultery against his wife is "aggravated" by the fact it was done with "a man of color." Gresham received further proof of her transgressions in 1831 after Sarah gave birth to a mulatto child. Gresham petitions for

divorce. In a lower court trial, Sarah Gresham accused her husband of being "incompetent to the discharge of his marital duties, of sexual intercourse." **Result:** rejected.

***

Petition 11683501
Virginia, Norfolk County
December 9, 1835-8 January 1836
Abstract: In 1831, Thomas Culpepper married Caroline Johnson. Shortly thereafter he accused her of being a "common prostitute, subject to the access of nearly all the young men in the town of Portsmouth." As prescribed in the 1827 law, Culpepper filed a statement concerning his wife's alleged behavior in the Clerk's Office, Norfolk County Circuit Superior Court of Law and Chancery, stating that Caroline "repeatedly associated with negroes" and engaged in carnal intercourse "with black men." He seeks a divorce. **Result:** rejected.

***

Petition 11683703
Virginia, King William County
March 5, 1837
Abstract: Elizabeth Pannell seeks a divorce from her husband, Edmund Pannell. Married at age sixteen, Elizabeth Pannell, who claims to be from "an ancient and respectable family," lost her entire estate when her husband squandered it "in all manner of dissipation." Accused of having committed a felony, Edmund Pannell was acquitted due to "irregularity in the proceedings" and fled from the county, leaving his wife destitute. In addition to being profligate, Pannell exhibited a cruel and abusive behavior toward his wife and engaged in "adultery and fornication" with black and white women, a fact known by all in the neighborhood. He even encouraged a slave named Grace, hired from Mrs. Louisa Deffarges and with whom he was conducting an adulterous affair, to be insolent toward his wife.

Result: referred to Committee for Courts of Justice.

***

Petition 11683835
Virginia, Orange County
January 29, 1838
Abstract: Richard Hall represents that his wife Sarah, "to your petitioners shame and mortification, was delivered of a colored child" after six month's marriage. Hall states that he "quitted the bed of she who had so [desecrated] him and has been from that time to this, a stranger to her." Citing that "since that time ... the said Sarah has had two other children both coloured," the petitioner prays "the legislature to disolve the union which connects him with one who has thus proven herself so unworthy."

Result: refereed to Committee for Courts of Justice.

***

Petition 11684008
Virginia, Nansemond County
December 14, 1840
Abstract: Bryant Rawls seeks a divorce from his wife, Rachel, who, after twelve years of marriage and three legitimate children, gave birth to a "colored child ... begotten by a negro." His wife abandoned him shortly afterwards, Rawls claims, and he is now caring for his own children and has placed the "mulatto" baby with a free black family.

Result: bill drawn.

***

Petition 11684104
Virginia, Frederick County
January 9-20, 1841

Abstract: Thomas Cain seeks a divorce from his wife Mary who has been guilty of adultery "of the most aggravated character the proof of which is found in the fact that on two separate occasions since her intermarriage ... Mary has been delivered and become the mother of black children who could not be other than the fruits of an adulterous intercourse with a negro."

Result: bill drawn.

***

Petition 11684105
Virginia, Preston County
December 9, 1841- 31 December 1842
Abstract: Jacob Plum asks for a divorce from his wife Mary Jane who a number of years prior to the filing of his petition gave birth to a mulatto child and continued to live with him until she recently abandoned their domicile. She has now been convicted of larceny and sent to the penitentiary.

Result: rejected.

***

Petition 11684106
Virginia, Campbell County
December 7-17, 1841
Abstract: After six years of separation, Sarah H. Robinson seeks a divorce. Her husband was cruel and tyrannical, drank to excess, and slept with numerous "lewd women, both white and black, and he had children by them." Finally he abandoned her and she has not seen him since that time.

Result: rejected.

***

Petition 11684311
Virginia, Culpeper County
January 18, 1843 - 27 February 1843
Abstract: Mary Lawry, the mother of four children by her husband Newsome Lawry, a convict in the penitentiary near

Richmond, seeks a divorce. In 1839, she informs the legislature, her husband began an "illicit intercourse" with a slave named Cynthia, the property of the estate of James Huffman and in the possession of the estate executor, Robert Huffman. Eventually Lawry stole a horse and fled with Cynthia to Wheeling, on their way, the petitioner supposes, to a free state. Cynthia was captured by Robert Huffman and the horse, though sold, was eventually recovered. Lawry returned to Richmond after Cynthia's capture and was arrested, convicted, and sent to prison.

Result: rejected.

Repository: Library of Virginia, Richmond, Virginia, Legislative Petitions

***

Petition 20184103
Alabama, Tallapoosa County 1841
Abstract: John Farley asks the court for a divorce from his wife, Mary. Anxious to derive happiness and contentment from his marriage, John says that, since their marriage in 1812, he has treated his wife with the utmost kindness and affection, providing for her "comfort & maintenance in sickness & in health." He states that for more than twenty years his wife was kind obedient and affectionate." But in the last three years her behavior toward has changed. She is now repaying his affection and good behavior with "cold and repulsive treatment," telling him that she desires "to get rid of your orator so that she might find some person more competent to the discharge of libidinous duties." Indeed, he says, when he became ill, Mary refused to call the family physician and laced his medicine with laudanum, fully aware of "the dangerous effects of over portions" of the drug. When they agreed to separate in 1839, John gave Mary a settlement of the property, including an improved lot in the town of Lafayette and a negro man named Lewis. By the next year, he states, Mary, "being wholly lost of her matrimonial obligations," engaged in adulterous affairs and

"was in the habits of daily prostituting herself." He seeks the return of property and slave that he put into trust for her support. **Result:** granted.

***

Petition 20184222
Alabama, Mobile County
April 15, 1842

Abstract: Margaret Garner has previously filed for a divorce and alimony from her husband Thomas Garner, a slave owner. In this bill, Garner states "that the said Thomas has become a bankrupt and has applied for the privilege of surrendering his property in discharge of his debts and he has thereby become unable to afford aid to your petitioner." Her own property "does not yield more than $12 per month." Citing abandonment and an adulterous affair on the part of her husband, Margaret prays for an allowance for her support during the divorce proceedings and for an allowance to pay the expenses of the court case. Two related petitions reveal that Thomas Garner, the owner of approximately sixteen slaves in 1841, was alleged to have taken a "mulattress to the bed" of his wife and to have "carnally Known" her.

Result: No recorded result.

***

Petition 20184306
Alabama, Sumter County
May 25, 1843

Abstract: Catharine Underwood seeks a divorce and property settlement from her husband Joel Underwood on the grounds of cruelty and adultery with a female slave. Six months into the marriage, Catharine reports, Joel "assumed a coldness and indifference towards her," which escalated to physical threats and abuse. In addition, she asserts that Joel commenced an "adulterous connexion" with a female slave he had purchased. Catharine charges that it was due to this illicit relationship that her husband "communicated to your oratrix a disease too loathsome and shocking to mention." She therefore asks the court for a divorce. **Result:** abated.

***

Petition 20184402
Alabama, Mobile County
October 11, 1844 - April 1845
Abstract: Maria Josephine Perier Saint Guirons seeks a divorce from her husband Pierre Saint Guirons on the grounds of cruelty and adultery with a "negro" woman. At the time of the marriage in 1831, Maria owned real and personal property worth over $20,000 while Pierre owned no property. Within four years, Pierre "had disposed of all her property," keeping the proceeds for himself. In addition, Maria charges that Pierre "was almost constantly intoxicated, and at times greatly illtreated and abused her." The petitioner further states that for the past eight years, Pierre has lived with a "negro" woman in an adulterous state which has resulted in the birth of several children. It is with "the deepest regret and mortification" that Maria petitions for divorce, citing that she "has lost a friend and protector with whom your Oratrix can never again feel free to cohabit."

Result: granted.

***

Petition 20184612
Alabama, Mobile County
April 11, 1846
Abstract: In 1844, at age fifteen, Catherine Awtry married Harvey Snow without her father's permission and "without her own consent being fully and freely and willingly given." A few months later, Catherine charges, Harvey went to the kitchen and remained there "until a late hour in the night in company with his negro woman." Later, she says, he engaged in "criminal intercourse and Sexual connection with his own Negro woman Slave in his own house and had a child by her the off spring of his illicit connection." Catherine

further charges that Harvey permitted the female slave "to abuse her in a most shameful and improper manner." In 1845, Harvey abandoned Catherine and migrated to Mississippi. When he returned, he went back to living with his slave and Catherine was forced from their home. Catharine asks for expenses to prosecute her suit, divorce and alimony.

Result: partially granted.

Repository: Bibb County Courthouse, Centreville, Alabama.

***

Petition 20184804
South Carolina, Abbeville County
September 25, 1848 - November 1852
Abstract: In 1818, Henry Norrell married Delila Calhoun in Abbeville District, South Carolina. A short time after their marriage his wife became obsessed with the idea that he was "having illicit intercourse" with one of his slaves, and eventually, to appease her, he sold the slave "at a very reduced price, & at great sacrifice." Later, he sold another woman for the same reason. In 1842, the couple moved to Alabama, where they farmed and raised a family of ten children. Now, he complains, they "do not lie on the same bed nor have any connection as man & wife" because of her jealousy and charges of adultery and "illicit connection[s] with other women." He has just discovered, however, that it is his wife who is guilty "of crimes of the foulest cast & of the blackest hue." Claiming that she is guilty of adultery with a man named Easterwood, and has given birth to another man's child, he asks for a divorce. **Result:** dismissed.

***

Petition 20184833
Alabama, Montgomery County
December 25, 1848

Abstract: On Christmas Day 1848, Albert G. Wray of Montgomery County, Alabama, sued his wife for divorce. Albert Wary had married Susan Mary Cox in 1833, in Georgia, and in 1842 they moved to Alabama. He continued to live with his wife until 15 October 1848, when he discovered that she was having a "carnal connection" with C. G. M. Prime, a portrait painter and physician. Albert asks the court to dissolve the marriage and issue a divorce decree. In her answer, Susan explains that she now lives in Oglethorp County, Georgia, with her mother. She had married Albert when she was "not exceeding sixteen years of age." She claims that, within six months of the marriage, his conduct became "cold, indifferent, distant, harsh and cruel ... better the relation of master and servant than husband & wife." He repeatedly "used violence ... shoving her down violently, boxing her jaws and face and committing other personal injuries on her body." A year after their marriage, she asserts, her husband began "a promiscuous illicit intercourse with his own negroe wenches and continued ... so long as complainant and defendant resided together, say for the space of fourteen years." Albert had in fact a special relationship with a female slave named Mary, a seamstress, who, Susan claims, bore him four "mulatto" children. In the summer and fall of 1843, Susan suffered mental breakdowns, and since then has "enjoyed but few lucid intervals." Her mental problems are a direct result of the cruel and inhuman treatment by her husband, she asserts. Now "ruined in mind, broken in Spirits," she is accused of adultery with C. G. M. Prime, "a drunken worthless vagabond" hired by her husband to "take advantage of defendant's mental imbecility." In her answer and counter-petitions, Susan reveals that her husband was the owner of eighty-five slaves, some of whom he had received upon his marriage to her. The related decree reveals that Susan was in fact in a mental institution by the time the court issued its decree in 1850.

Result: None found.

***

Petition 20184912
Alabama, Montgomery County
July 1849
Abstract: Susan M. Wray, living with her mother Mary Cox in Lexington, Georgia, complains that the two female slaves her husband gave her to support herself during their divorce proceedings have left without her permission. They are now in "the possession & control" of her husband, Albert Wray, she says; and consequently, during April, May, and June, she lost sixty-five dollars they would have earned as hired slaves. Susan asks for that amount and additional funds to pay her attorney's fees.

Result: No recorded result.

***

Petition 20184915
Alabama, Montgomery County
May 14, 1849
Abstract: Several related petitions reveal that in 1848, Albert Wray had filed divorce from his wife, Susan Mary Wray on grounds of adultery with one C. G. M. Prime, a portrait painter and physician. Susan Mary Wray had countercharged that her husband had treated her cruelly and had ongoing illicit intercourse with his slaves, and specifically with a seamstress named Mary who had given birth to several mulatto children. In this answer and cross bill, Albert G. Wray denies that he treated his wife Susan "with a spirit of unkindness harshness cruelty and neglect;" he denies that he had illicit sexual relations with any of his slaves; and he denies encouraging C. G. M. Prince to seduce his wife so that he (Wray) could file a petition for divorce. He defends himself against charges of illicit intercourse with the slave Mary by stating that "There is one of the children of the said Mary about two years old who is the reputed child of a bright mulattoe slave called John." Whether her other children are

mulattos, he explains, is difficult to know, but he is sure about one thing: none of them are his.

Result: No recorded result.

***

Petition 20185009
Alabama, Montgomery County
January18 - February 22, 1850

Abstract: In this supplemental bill, Susan M. Wray repeats many of the arguments she has previously put forth in her answer to her husband's 1848 petition for divorce: her husband, Albert Wray, is a man of wealth worth perhaps fifty thousand dollars; he owns a large number of slaves, and has the means to provide her with added support although he refuses to do so. But now, she explains, she has been committed to a lunatic asylum in Columbia, South Carolina, suffering from paroxysms of derangement. She needs her husband's financial assistance immediately and asks the court to "decree further allowances."

Result: granted.

***

Petition 20185012
Alabama, Montgomery County
August 1, 1850

Abstract: This petition is one of several petitions filed by Susan Wray in response to her husband's 1848 suit for divorce on the grounds of adultery. Susan complained that "no provision whatever exists for her support, while the suit shall be pending & until all the matters & things in controversy shall be finally settled." Although the court has awarded Susan alimony in the amount of $650, and four hundred dollars in lawyer's fees, it has been twenty months and she has spent the money. Since there is no provision made for her future support, Susan asks for additional payments. Several related petitions reveal that Susan had been committed to a lunatic asylum, and was still there as of 1850. The Chancellor's decree to Susan's plea: "If there could have existed any doubt on the subject previous to the unfortunate occurrence, which caused this suit the present undisputed insanity of Mrs Wray, now an inmate of a lunatic asylum, the testimony of the eminent Superintending physician of that institution; and the particular form and manifestation of her lunacy, demonstrate to my mind at least, beyond the shadow of a doubt, that for many years prior to the institution of this suit, she has not been a morally responsible being; and that probably at the time of her marriage her mind was disordered-- that this fatal infirmity was progressive in its character and gradually increased until all her facilities and perceptions, reason, will and moral sense, became the helpless instruments of insane impulse and delusion."

Result: No recorded result.

***

Petition 20185109
Alabama, Mobile County
February 25, 1851
Abstract: Tabitha Pope charges that her husband, William Oswald Pope, committed frequent acts of adultery with women of color. In 1849, he engaged in an illicit relationship with Violet, a black woman owned by his father-in-law; and in 1850 and 1851, he had "carnal connection[s]" with his own slave, a "certain Mulatto woman named Maria Jane." According to a related testimony, in the late evening, Pope would go to the shop where Maria Jane lived, enter her quarters, take "off his boots & stockings & breeches & completely undress himself," put out the lamp, and light a candle. Tabitha also charges that her husband frequently cursed her in "the most insulting and opprobrious terms." The insults, Tabitha says, were worse "than the infliction of personal violence, because they were outrages upon her womanly delicacy and sensibility." In 1851, she sues for divorce, citing infidelity and cruelty.

Result: dismissed.

***

Petition 20185212
Alabama, Dallas County
April 1852 - June 1853
Abstract: In 1841, Jane M. Potter, daughter of a prosperous Wilcox County plantation owner, married William Bizzell, an overseer with little means. Jane's father gave the couple a "valuable negro Boy aged about Seven years," a horse, saddle, bedding and other items "Necessary for young persons beginning in life with but little property." During the next decade, Bizzell, described as a man of "great energy & unwearied industry," acquired a number land and a number of slaves. Among the slaves was "a negro woman of light complexion named Mary with whom he was keeping up a criminal connection." He became so infatuated with her and so "open in his intercourse" that in 1844 he vowed he would "never part with this woman." Bizzell and Mary had two mulatto children. Bizzell also had four children by his wife, four of whom had died by the time she filed her petition. In 1845, Jane left and filed for divorce. Fearful of losing some of his property, Bizzell sought to appease his wife by sending the slave Mary to Ohio and promising to reform. But after she dropped her suit and returned home in 1848, he grew increasingly violent and carried on an illicit relationship with another of his slaves named Polly. In order to avoid suspicion, Jane Claims, her husband selected Polly specifically because she had a husband. Jane again left him, and again filed for divorce and alimony. Bizzell, who had sold most of his property, except for eight slaves, fled from the state. He died before a decree was rendered in the case.

Result: abated.

***

Petition 20185620
Alabama, Mobile County
October 11, 1856

Abstract: Caroline Stevens seeks a divorce from her husband Nathaniel, who, she says, "voluntarily left her and her children and took up with a certain negro woman." Although he owns property and makes a good income as one of the best river pilots in Mobile, Caroline claims that her husband spends his income on "himself and his colored concubine." She asks the court to require him to provide "for the support of herself and children" who "are in danger of being subjected to shame degradation & absolute want" and to prevent him from otherwise disposing of his property. Related testimony reveals that Nathaniel Stevens lived in the same house as one Mary Malone, a woman of "mixed" color. Stevens reportedly paid rent for the house. Mary Malone lived which her mother and a nine-year-old boy. **Result:** granted.

***

Petition 20185853
Alabama, Sumter County
June 12, 1858
Abstract: In an earlier related petition, Mary Ann Merriman had filed for divorce from William Merriman, citing as reasons his intoxication and abusive behavior. To bolster her case she now adds that William is also guilty of adultery with a number of slave women, including Polly, Amanda, Emily, Rachael, and "other negro women whose names and description are unknown to your oratrix." In her original bill of complaint, Mary Ann informed the court that, at the time of her marriage to William Merriman, she was a widow possessed of property that included a "copper" colored slave named Polly. Although not specifically stated, assumption has been made that the Polly cited in the amended bill is the Polly owned by Mary Ann prior to her marriage to William Merriman. Assumption has also been made that the other three slaves mentioned in the amended bill were held by William Merriman. **Result:** dismissed.

***

Petition 20185926
Alabama, Mobile County
March 26, 1859

Abstract: Isabella A. Kelly, married since 1839, claims that in the mid-1840s she discovered that her husband, physician Edwin H. Kelly, was having "constant and undisguised" sex with a slave he owned named Matilda. She contends that Matilda gave birth to two of his children. Isabella left Edwin on several occasions, but always came back when the doctor promised to reform his character. Following their first separation, she began acquiring "separate property," with her husband acting as her agent and trustee. She bought and sold slaves, hired them out, and purchased real estate. With the profits of her various transactions, she purchased a rental house, putting up cash and two as down payment. All the while, she claims, her husband treated her unkindly, forced her to live in uncomfortable circumstances in the hospital where he practiced medicine, and took the profits from her property. In 1859, she finally separated and files a bill of complaint, charging that her husband has taken control of her property. Through a "next friend," she asks the court to remove him from "the trusteeship, management & control of her separate property," and also prays for "proper alimony." In his lengthy answer to the charges, Edwin Kelly gives a very different picture of the marriage, describing his wife as a woman constantly dissatisfied and jealous of every female in their entourage. He accuses her of cruelty toward a slave, stealing his money and trying to defraud him. He denies the charges of adultery and countercharges that his wife has denied him marital right for many years.

Result: No recorded result.

***

Petition 20186033
Alabama, Dallas County
January 23, 1860-61

Abstract: In 1860, Mary Jane Davis, twenty-three years old, sues for divorce from her forty-five-year-old husband, Daniel, a farmer. Mary Jane claims that, shortly after their marriage in 1858, she discovered that her husband "was living in adulterous intercourse with a [hired] slave named Dice," owned by Sarah Blalock. Mary Jane contends that her husband stayed with Dice "until late hours of the Night in the house where she stayed and on one night he remained [there] all night." Moreover, Mary Jane was not permitted to keep the keys to the farmhouse, smokehouse, or other buildings, as they were turned over to Dice. Unable to endure the humiliation, she moved away, while Daniel continued "to carry out his criminal purposes," hiring Dice in 1859 and 1860, and living alone with her on his farm. In his answer to his wife's bill of complaint, Daniel Davis emphatically denies the charge of adultery with Dice or with any other slave. He informs the court that such an act would be against nature given the fact that his wife is young, healthy and very handsome, while Dice is over fifty year of age and has children and grandchildren. He claims that his wife has abandoned him because he has insufficient means, and she has told him so.

Result: dismissed.

***

Petition 20186702
Alabama, Henry County
September 17, 1867 - 7 May 1868

Abstract: Simon Farmer, a man of color, seeks a divorce from his wife, Sally, who, he claims, abandoned his "bed & board, & has since that time committed adultery with one James Paramon, Colored, &, others." He asks the court to subpoena his wife, who, he believes, is living in Georgia.

Result: granted.

***

Petition 20482604
District of Colombia, Washington, County
July 10, 1826

Abstract: Ann Gibson charges her husband, Gerard Gibson, with "drunkeness and debauchery." She complains of his violent temper and accuses him of sleeping with "a negress." Ann Gibson asks for "such alimony & seperate maintenance . . . as from the fortune she brought to her said husband." She also asks for an injunction to prevent her husband from further selling any of her property, including the remainder of her thirteen slaves.

Result: partially granted.

***

Petition 20486103
District of Colombia, Washington, County
January19 - 27 May 1861

Abstract: Rhoda Strother seeks a divorce from her husband, Dr. Robert Strother, on the grounds of adultery. She states that shortly after their marriage in 1856, she suspected him of adulterous activities. At one point, she "saw him kiss a woman of bad reputation at a public hotel in the City of St. Louis." Shortly thereafter, she received a letter from another woman, telling her that Dr. Strother "sought her company, and that she repulsed him, because, bad as she was, she did not wish to take a husband from a young wife." Mrs. Strother then contracted a serious illness and was forced to leave their home in the District of Columbia to recuperate in Virginia. When she returned, Mrs. Strother received an anonymous letter stating that Dr. Strother planned to meet a "negro woman" at the petitioner's house. Mrs. Strother "concealed herself in a closet, and at nearly the time named, the woman came into the room in Mrs. Gaines' house, used by Dr Strother as an office, attached to which was the said closet. Dr Strother met the woman as Your Petitioner plainly saw, took her into the parlor and was seen sitting with her upon the sofa with her hand in his for a long time." When the woman left, Mrs. Strother followed her and confronted her. She states that the woman "informed your Petitioner that Dr Strother had threatened to kill her if she betrayed their criminal intercourse to his wife." The woman further informed the petitioner that she was supposed to meet Dr. Strother later that evening. The petitioner then "obtained a white witness" and concealed herself and the witness in the closet. When the "negress" arrived, "your Petitioner heard him tell her what to say the next morning when she was to be brought before your Petitioner, and threatened her with violence if she should confess to your Petitioner their Criminal intercourse." Mrs. Strother revealed herself from her hiding place, confronted her husband, and left the house. The petitioner states that Dr. Strother moved to Kansas Territory. He filed for and obtained a divorce on the grounds of desertion. She avers that these charges are false and requests a divorce on the grounds of adultery. In addition, the petitioner seeks custody of her son and wishes to maintain control of her property.

Result: granted.

***

Petition 20486255
District of Colombia, Washington
January 4 – 12 June 1862
Abstract: Kate McConnell seeks a divorce from her husband, Dr. James McConnell, on the grounds of adultery. She avers that her husband confessed to committing adultery with a "person, or woman of bad repute." In addition, she was informed that he was "too intimate with one of the chambermaids, a negro woman." Mrs. McConnell states that after receiving this information, she concealed herself in a room adjoining her husband's room and overheard a conversation between Dr. McConnell and the chambermaid. "The Said Dr. James McConnell made propositions to her, saying he wanted to stay with her while his wife was absent and advanced towards her and caught hold of her; She told him his wife was in the adjoining room,

and would hear him." The petitioner then revealed herself and rebuked her husband. Mrs. McConnell further states that following this incident, she went to visit some friends in Virginia. While she was there, she had an accident which caused her to give premature birth and become very ill. Her husband was notified, but Mrs. McConnell avers that he stayed only four or five days with her. Dr. McConnell traveled for some time before writing the petitioner and informing her that he was establishing a practice in Cleveland, Ohio. Mrs. McConnell then received reports that Dr. McConnell "had commenced his 'old practices,' of living, and cohabiting with persons or women of notorious bad moral character." She prays for a divorce and the restoration of her maiden name.

Result: granted.

***

Petition 20584201
Florida, Leon County
August 16, 1842
Abstract: Sarah M. Whiting seeks a divorce from her husband, Francis B. Whiting. Explaining that she was between fourteen and fifteen years old when she married, she adds that soon afterwards "to her surprise and mortification she ascertained that her said husband was unfaithful to her and habitually indulged in illicit intercourse with a female slave whom he owned and retained about his house." She left him, but offered to return if her husband would remove the female slave. He agreed, telling her that the slave had been sold, but she eventually discovered that the slave was simply residing in another house owned by her husband. When she confronted him about his continued relationship with the slave "he replied that he would do as he pleased and persisted in the most open and shameless manner in living in adultery with said slave." She left and now files for divorce and alimony. **Result:** No recorded result.

***

Petition 20680602
Georgia, Greene County
1806
Abstract: Mary Jackson, the wife of Joseph Jackson, asks by her next friend Samuel Beckum [Buckan] that her husband be required to appear and show cause, if any, why her plea for a divorce should not be granted. Mary states that she has been an obedient wife but that Joseph has "lived in the habitual indulgance of carnal commerce" and the "daily commision of Addultery" with a "negro woman" whom he owns. He has "countenanced & permited" the slave to beat and whip his wife. He has been adulterous with other women as well, both black and white. Moreover, Joseph has treated Mary in a cruel manner and has banished her from his home. **Result:** No recorded result.

***

Petition 20685316
Georgia, Richmond County
February 9, 1853 - 1855
Abstract: Johnson Clark Abbot and Eliza M. Abbot were married on 25 October 1842. On 1 October 1850, Clark Abbot left their house and has not been seen again. Eliza Abbot also claims that since the desertion, Clark Abbot is "given to habitual intoxication, that he still remains the victim of intemperance & as such has become so depraved, that he has been exiled from the society of white persons & his associates are now negroes with whom [he] carouses & is in the daily habit of getting drunk & that he has at various times had carnal connection with other women." Eliza Abbot seeks a divorce.

Result: granted.

***

Petition 20783713
Kentucky, Harrison County
October 3, 1837
Abstract: Rachel Mullins states that she was married to William Turner, with whom she had twelve children. Following his death, she married Henry Mullins, but he soon "became cruel and morose ... and your oratrix has been compelled to leave his house." She further charges that Henry has kept "one of his own negro woman as a concubine by whom he has children and lives in a state of open concubinage." Her father's estate is about to be distributed, and Rachel fears Henry will take her share of the estate and leave her and her children without support. She asks that Henry be enjoined from taking her inheritance and that he be required to repay her the personal estate of her first husband.

Result: No recorded result.

***

Petition 20784606
Kentucky, Pike County
March 18, 1846 - April 7, 1847
Abstract: John King contends that while he was working in Pikeville, his wife, Sally "went off with one Leonard Sexton a half-Negro and lived in adultery in the basest manner." Sally returned "after her base and unpardonable actions." She left again with Sexton after having his child. Sally, Sexton, and the baby have gone to the state of Virginia. King seeks a divorce, "restoring him from all obligations of so debased a woman and reinstating him to all the privileges of an unmarried man."

Result: Granted.

***

Petition 20784713
Kentucky, Boyle County

October 4, 1847- September 1848

Abstract: Permelia Russell, free woman of color, seeks a divorce from Willis, a former slave who was freed after the death of his owner, Robert Craddock. Permelia states Willis behaves towards her in a cruel and inhuman manner. After a two-week visit with her mother in Louisville, "she returned home, and to her great surprise found that the Deft had rented out their residence to a white family," and he "left [their furniture and clothing] in charge of the family." Permelia charges that the family refused to let her collect her possessions. She states Willis holds "about five thousand dollars worth of property," consisting of a house and lot in Danville, KY, worth $1,500; land in Casey, KY, worth $2,000; and other property worth $1,500. Permelia seeks alimony and support from Willis. [Five people gave depositions wherein they testified that they had lived with the Russells, were neighbors of the Russells, or had known one or both of them for a long period time. For these reasons, it was presumed that these individuals were free people of color.]

Result: dismissed.

***

Petition 20882632
Louisiana, West Baton Rouge Parish
30 November 1826 - November 29, 1830

Abstract: Margaret Constance Richard seeks a separation of property and of bed and board from her husband, Alexander McDougald. Margaret claims that, although she has been a "kind faithful, prudent and affectionate wife," her husband has "treated her in a cruel, outrageous, dishonorable and inhuman manner, so as to render her living with him longer insupportable." Margaret informs the court that McDougald has assaulted her on several occasions and tried to kill her. In addition, he has publicly defamed her character by calling her a "damned bitch," a whore, and "accusing her of sleeping with negroes, meaning thereby that your petitioner had been guilty of having criminal connexion with negroes." At the time of their 1810 marriage,

Margaret owned considerable property including a plantation and several slaves. She thus asks to have the property she brought into the marriage restored to her, for a division of the property acquired during their marriage, and for a separation from bed and board.

Result: granted; partly granted; appealed; appeal granted.

***

Petition 20882808
Louisiana, St. Landry, Parish
May 5 - 31, 1828
Abstract: Victorine Ledeé, a free man of color, seeks a divorce from his wife, Honorine Matté, a free woman of color. Ledeé represents that he has been married to Honorine for five or six years and, during that time, he has "always conducted himself with property" and furnished his wife with "all those necessaties which his limited means would permit." However, in the past six months, Honorine has repeatedly committed adultery with "many different men and particularly with François Simien also a free man of color." On these grounds, Ledeé seeks a divorce and custody of the couple's two minor children. **Result:** dismissed.

***

Petition 20882837
Louisiana, Iberville, Parish
April 28 - September 23, 1828
Abstract: Pauline Bergeron seeks a separation of bed and board from her husband, Baptiste Bergeron. Pauline claims that, upon her marriage, she brought a dowry of $1,500. In addition, she complains that Baptiste has been "repeatedly guilty of excesses, cruel treatment and outrages" against her. She further claims that he has had "frequent and illicit connexion with the negro women slaves," compelling her to "bring up and support his spurious offspring by the said slaves." Pauline also charges that her husband has

committed "violent assault and battery" upon her while she was "in an advanced state of pregnancy." She claims that the outrages committed against her have made living with Baptiste "insupportable and dangerous." She prays that an inventory and appraisal be made of all their community property. She also asks for an order directing her husband to return her dowry and enjoining him from disposing of any part of the property until the suit has been settled. Finally, she prays that she and her husband be separated in bed and board and that he be condemned to pay support for her and their minor children.

Result: dismissed.

***

Petition 20882913
Louisiana, St. Landry Parish
May18 - June 6, 1829
Abstract: Jean Baptiste Guillory, a free man of color, seeks a divorce from his wife, Marguerite Caraballo, a free woman of color. Guillory asserts that, though he has always been "a good and affectionate husband," Marguerite "has been guilty of repeated acts of adultery with different persons and particularly with a coloured & married man named George Simien." Jean Baptiste claims that Marguerite abandoned him and their five children about six months ago and has continued to commit adultery since then. Guillory prays for a divorce from Marguerite "& that he & she may be placed in the same situation as tho' no marriage had ever been contracted between them." In addition, he prays for custody of the children as his wife "has proven herself unworthy of Keeping & raising them."

Result: granted.

***

Petition 20883314
Louisiana, Orleans, Parish
August 7, 1833 – March 14, 1835

Abstract: Maria W. Webb charges that the verbal and physical abuse she has received, over the years, at the hands of her husband, as well as the reality of his adulterous connection with one of their slaves named Nancy, has driven her and her children out of their "common dwelling." Maria claims that William, whom she married in 1809 in England, has "pursued towards her a course of excess, cruel treatment and outrage," beating her, calling her names "too disgusting to be mentioned," and allowing the slave Nancy to behave with "insolence & abuse" toward her. Maria Webb seeks alimony at the rate of $30 per month and a separation of "bed and board." She also prays for a decree of "partition" of their common property, which consists of land, household furniture, stocks in a "bottling establishment," and six slaves. In the meantime, she prays for an order enjoining her husband from selling the property.

Result: granted.

***

Petition 20883823
Louisiana, East Baton Rouge Parish
May 18, 1838 - January 12, 1839
Abstract: Elizabeth Bills prays to be separated from her husband of five years, Hugh M. Blake. Elizabeth represents that Hugh's "Excesses," ill treatment, and adulterous conduct have made their living together "insupportable." She alleges that Hugh has called her "a damn mulatto Bitch" and abandoned her, boasting that "he had other women to take care of." Elizabeth therefore asks the court to grant her a separation in "bed & board" from her husband and prays for a judgment of "final divorce."

Result: partially granted; plea of reconvention

***

Petition 20884115

Louisiana Orleans Parish
April 31, 1841- June 12, 1841
Abstract: V. Hubert Dénisse seeks a divorce from his wife Eugénie Duenrabe. Dénisse represents that Eugénie, who has never "conducted herself with decency and propriety," left the "matrimonial domicile" in 1837 or 1838, and stole away in the dead of the night with a man of color. He contends that she has since been living in Mobile in a state of "concubinage" with the said man of color. Dénisse claims that he has invited Eugénie to return to him, but she has refused. He therefore asks for a separation of bed and board, followed by a divorce. **Result:** granted.

***

Petition 20884719
Louisiana St. Landry Parish
February 5, 1847- June 4, 1849
Abstract: Jane Davis, a free mulatto woman, seeks to be "separated in bed and board" from her husband, William Edmunds, a free man of color. The couple intermarried in 1835 and "lived together happily and contentedly" for many years. Notwithstanding her "dutiful and affectionate" behavior, Jane now charges that William has broken his "marital vows" by abandoning, deceiving, and maltreating her, and that he is at the moment in "the embraces" of another woman. Moreover, William now denies that he and Jane were ever "united in the bonds of Lawful wedlock," thus publicly "defaming and blackening" his wife's reputation. He even induces people to believe that Jane is "of doubtful fame & chastity." Jane asserts that their living together is insupportable; she therefore seeks a separation from her husband and financial support during her "natural life." Related depositions provide detailed information about life among free people of color in Philadelphia, where Jane lived for some time.

Result: motion to dismiss.

***

Petition 20884846
Louisiana Orleans Parish
November 9, 1848
Abstract: Mary Amelia Wilson, widow of Joseph W. Tisdale, seeks a writ of sequestration for a woman of color named Louisa and for Louisa's seven-year-old daughter named Lydia. Mary Amelia Tisdale represents that Louisa was given to her by her father as dowry and is therefore her property. Mrs. Tisdale charges that, about seven years ago, her late husband took Louisa from her and led her to believe that the slave had been removed to Texas and sold. Louisa's mulatto mother, whom Mary Amelia also claims as her slave, is in fact still in Texas, held by one Albert C. Horton. As for Louisa, however, Mrs. Tisdale has just discovered that she is not in Texas, but in New Orleans where she was living as Joseph Tisdale's concubine and passing for a white free person. Mary Amelia Wilson Tisdale therefore seeks a writ of sequestration for Louisa and Lydia, and asks the court to declare them her property. She also seeks to gain ownership of Louisa's personal belongings, which include some furniture.

Result: partially granted.

***

Petition 20885513
Louisiana Orleans Parish
March 26, 1855 - June 22, 1857
Abstract: Francis Terence, a free man of color, seeks a divorce from his wife of four years, Josephine Johnson, also a free woman of color. Terence represents that Josephine's conduct since the marriage has been "such as to render it insupportable for him to live with her any longer." Francis charges that his wife's "habits" are dissolute, that she frequents "Houses of prostitution" and "lewd Ballrooms," that she has committed adultery with Eugene Milleur and lives with him in "open concubinage," that she has received Milleur in the marital bed, that she has contracted a venereal

disease, and that she has clandestinely left the conjugal "domicil." Francis Terence therefore prays that his wife be cited to answer his petition and that a judgment of divorce be "pronounced" against her. **Result:** granted.

***

Petition 20984410
Maryland Baltimore County
February 3, 1844 - March 2, 1846
Abstract: Henry Houck seeks to end his three-year marriage with his wife, Eleanora, because she has committed adultery. Houck explains that Eleanora admitted her infidelities to him, and he has "resolved never again to receive her as his wife" and has sent her to live with her father. He asks the court to subpoena her to answer these charges and to a decree a divorce. A related deposition from Donaldson Forster describes his sexual encounters with the defendant that were arranged by "a coloured man named Rice." According to Forster, several of these appointments took place "at different times on the same day" upstairs at Rice's house.

Result: granted.

***

Petition 20984501
Maryland Baltimore County
July 21 - December 17, 1845
Abstract: Elizabeth Collins and William Collins were married in 1826 and had three children. After seven years of marriage, her "husband ceased to give any support to your petitioner or her children." He separated from his wife and they have lived apart for the last eleven years while Elizabeth has supported herself and the children. In 1845, William Collins returned to Baltimore "and is now residing in said City with a mulatto woman who holds to him the

relation, de facto, of wife." The petitioner asks the court to subpoena her husband to issue a divorce decree. In a supplemental bill filed three months later, she claims that William Collins never answered the summons and asks the court to issue an interlocutory decree.

Result: partially granted.

***

Petition 21085631
Mississippi Adams County
April 9, 1856 - May 18, 1857
Abstract: Lydia Jane Ireson states that she married Lansford O. Ireson in 1846. She now charges that the said Lansford "wickedly disregarding the solemnity of his vows, and the Sanctity of the marriage state hath committed adultery at divers times with one Lucy a woman of colour, and other women to your oratrix unknown." Lydia further represents that her said husband also "committed adultery, with a woman of colour, by the name of Caroline, on the said Plantation of your oratrix." The petitioner therefore prays that "the marriage between your Oratrix and the said Lansford O Ireson may be dissolved."

Result: granted.

***

Petition 21085704
Mississippi Jefferson County
October 14, 1857
Abstract: Louisa Hamberlin charges her husband Thomas with "frequent Acts of Adultery - with a Certain negro woman slave - named Cora" and that "he has committed said adultery in the same room where Complainant was -- in the most offensive and indecent manner." Asserting that her husband's illicit relationship took place from 1853-57, Louisa also confides that her husband "has had issue one child by said Cora during said marriage which said child he openly and notoriously claims as his by said Cora." The petitioner

therefore prays for "a decree divorcing her from the Bonds of matrimony."

Result: No recorded result.

***

Petition 21085808
Mississippi Claiborne County
March15 - April 8, 1858
Abstract: Susanah Bailey asks the court to grant her a divorce. She charges her husband, Henry M. Bailey, with a "wanton, deliberate and systematic course of cruelty and ill-treatment." She also charges her husband with adultery "with and upon a certain negro woman named Clara" in March of 1858. A witness deposes that he saw Clara and Henry Bailey "lying on the ground, said defendant being on top of said negro woman -- she having her clothes up -- evidently engaged in having sexual intercourse" in the horse lot. The deposition also reveals that Henry seized another "negro woman" around the waist but said woman struggled "a little, saying to him to let her go -- that she would not do it."

Result: granted.

***

Petition 21085813
Mississippi Claiborne County
April 22 - September 9, 1858
Abstract: Caroline Dungan asks the court to grant her a divorce from her husband, Jacob Dungan. The petitioner discloses that two years ago her husband "committed the crime of adultery with a certain negro slave," confiding that Jacob has "openly and notoriously lived apart from your Oratrix, and in adultery with said negro slave, with whom he has constantly committed, and still does daily commit, the crime of adultery." The complainant seeks to dissolve her marriage and asks the court to order her husband to answer

her charges. Witnesses deposed in the case state that Jacob Dungan freely admitted his adulterous relationship with the "mulatto woman named Sarah" and acknowledged as his own her two children, who are "as white as any white children, with straight hair." Witnesses also state that Dungan told them that he had freed Sarah and her children. **Result:** granted.

***

Petition 21085912
Mississippi Lowndes County
May 13, 1859
Abstract: Elizabeth R. Askew charges her husband Napoleon B. Askew with living "an adulterous life" with a mulatto woman named Catherine Rebecca, and she seeks a divorce from said Napoleon since he has "lost the disposition and power to care and provide for the moral and also the physical wants of his wife and children." The petitioner further argues that the provisions made by him for the support of his daughters is insufficient. Elizabeth therefore prays for "divorce and alimony and the care, custody and maintenance of the children" as well as "for such relief and for such orders and decrees in the premises as to your Honor may under the circumstances seem meet and proper." Napoleon's drunkenness and debauchery is "notorious" in the neighborhood.

Result: granted.

***

Petition 21184216
Missouri Boone County
April 25, 1842
Abstract: Robert Chiles seeks a divorce from his wife Celia. He submits that the said Celia has been "guilty of the crime of Adultery with certain & divers persons whose names to your orator are unknown." He further cites that "she has very frequently offered such indignities to his person as to render his Condition intolerable so much so that he was compelled

to absent himself from his own home." Revealing that "she has been guilty of Adultery since his separation from her and was impregnated by a negro man," the petitioner prays that the court will "render a decree dissolving the bonds of matrimony between him & Celia and restore to him all the rights & priviledges of a single man."

Elizabeth Caton stated in her deposition that Celia "had a child and ... that the child was born and was a dark mullato color and ... that she asked her who was the gather of the child and She [Celia] answered and said that he was a negro by the name of Abram who belonged to the widow adams."

Result: unknown.

***

Petition 21200001
North Carolina Nash County
Date not specified
Abstract: Thomas Flowers seeks a divorce from his wife Temperance, who "has taken up and cohabitted with people of colour, by whom she has had a child of colour & mixed blood, and with whom she has long associated."

Result: granted.

***

Petition 21281501
North Carolina Stokes County
October 10, 1815
Abstract: Married in 1811, Hannah Hussey charges that her husband Thomas treated her with great cruelty. He sided with the slaves who took "improper Liberties" with her; and he sided with Rachel, the free black wife of his slave Jack, who was insolent and abusive towards her. In addition, the slaves and Rachel lived upstairs in the Hussey house, and according to one witness, "made Such a dirt, & stink, that She could not beare it." "She in vain demanded of him the protection to which she was entitled," Hannah wrote, "the Comfort which he had pledged his Honour to bestow." In the

end, he forced her to leave, even as she was about to give birth to his child. She seeks alimony and support.

Result: No recorded result.

***

Petition 21281803
North Carolina Richmond County
June 30, 1818
Abstract: After two years of marriage, Jane Robinson seeks a divorce, charging that her husband William Robinson engaged in "promiscuous cohabitation with various women of loose and immoral habits" including slaves. Several related depositions reveal a pattern of unwelcomed sexual advances thrust by William Robinson upon the female slaves of various acquaintances.

Result: No recorded result.

***

Petition 21282001
North Carolina Stokes County
1820
Abstract: James Larimore seeks a divorce from his wife Catharine, a woman with "abandoned" habits who engaged in "adulterous intercourse with diverse individuals." He accused her of having sex with a mulatto man named William Goings during the night she sat up with the dying wife of a neighbor; he accused her of having an affair with one of his slaves in their kitchen; and he accused her of having illicit connections with a white man named Joseph Pane. In addition, she had "gone off to the State of Indianna."

Result: No recorded result.

***

Petition 21282403

North Carolina Perquimans County
April 1824
Abstract: Sarah Oneel seeks a divorce and alimony from her husband William Oneel, who, she contends, has abused her and mistreated her for many years. Not only did he beat and threaten to kill her, but in 1822 he took away their only child, a four-year-old daughter. Now he is "living in a vile & infamous state of adultery with a black woman whom he purchased for the purpose of keeping as his mistress."

Result: No recorded result

***

Petition 21282803
North Carolina Craven County
November 13, 1828
Abstract: Graham Bishop asks for a divorce from his wife Zilphia Stokes Bishop, who, he charges, was guilty of "a species of prostitution" before their marriage, and intimate with a slave named Brister afterwards. Currently, he says, she is living in open adultery with another man in New Bern, professing "to be his true and lawful wife."

Result: No recorded result.

***

Petition 21282904
North Carolina Chatham County
February 12, 1829
Abstract: A person of "Strict morality and Virtue," Rachel Hamlet, daughter of the late George Hamlet, asks for a divorce from William Hamlet, who, she asserts, lives a life of "riot and dissipation" engaging in "the most shameful and notorious habits of fornication and adultery" with "women of all classes and colour."

Result: No recorded result.

***

Petition 21283003
North Carolina Guilford County
October 27, 1830

Abstract: In 1823, Andrew Whittington, a young boy, married Lucy Whittington, an older woman who remained with him only a few months before moving back to her mother's house. Andrew found it difficult to live alone and he too moved back to his mother's. During the next three years, "being not yet grown," Andrew lived with "other families." Later, he convinced Lucy to return and they lived together for about ten months, Lucy giving birth to a baby. After the birth, however, she again left, and he has not seen or heard from her since. Andrew charges that in the past few years Lucy has engaged in "criminal intercourse" with whites and blacks, has given birth to two illegitimate children, and has been seen in bed with Ned Gawer, a free man of color. He seeks a divorce.

Result: No recorded result.

***

Petition 21283105
North Carolina Perquimans County
October 1831

Abstract: In 1829, after four years of marriage and three children, Gabriel Goodwin explains that his wife, Mary Lane Goodwin, "brought forth her fourth child which to your petitioners utter confusion and dismay was a dark [mulatto] and one half negro." A short time later, Goodwin left his wife, and now seeks a divorce. **Result:** No recorded result.

***

Petition 21283109
North Carolina Granville County
March 20, 1831

Abstract: In 1823, after six years of marriage, Charles Mitchell discovered that his wife Susan was "engaged in a shameful and adulterous intercourse with one Jo Proctor a freeman of color." Mitchell left his wife, and moved to Milton, North Carolina. Later, he learned that she and Proctor began a journey to Georgia, but for some reason abandoned their plans. She then followed him to Milton, took up residence "in the suburbs," and, for two years, "engaged in a course of shameless prostitution." He seeks a divorce.

Result: No recorded result.

***

Petition 21283110
North Carolina Granville County
September 1831

Abstract: In 1823, after eighteen years of marriage, William Hickman began to suspect that the children born during their union were not his. Even after he became convinced that this was the case, he did not file for divorce, hoping to avoid humiliating members of his wife's family "who were numerous & respectable." Finally, in 1827, however, Hickman discovered that "a mulatto slave, living in the neighborhood" had fathered his children. Hickman seeks a divorce. **Result:** No recorded result.

***

Petition 21283301
North Carolina, Wake County
April 4, 1833

Abstract: Elisha Lee seeks a divorce from his wife Elizabeth who falsely accused him of committing adultery with a black woman. He explains that Elizabeth "ran away and deserted him" in 1828, and despite his efforts, he failed to bring her back. "I ascribed her dislike to me to her great love of the bottle," he wrote, and the baleful influence of her mother. Later, he discovered that she gave birth to a mulatto baby. "I saw the child," he said, "and have no hesitation in saying that I believe it is a coloured child."

Result: No recorded result.

***

Petition 21283303
North Carolina Wake County
July 29, 1833
Abstract: Elizabeth Smith seeks a divorce and alimony from her husband Zachariah Smith, who, she charges, is abusive and cruel. Shortly after giving birth to a child, he beat her and forced her to leave their house, accusing her of giving birth to a mulatto baby "begotten by a free man of color." She asks the court to prevent him from running off with the eight slaves she brought to their marriage as she has learned that "a negro speculator is to go to the house of said Smith on tomorrow for the purpose of purchasing & secretly carrying off said slaves." **Result:** No recorded result.

***

Petition 21283304
North Carolina Craven County
August 12, 1833
Abstract: In 1824, after obtaining a license, free blacks Henry Richardson and Mary McQuinn were married in Craven County. Now, nine years later, Henry charges that he is not the father of one of their five children, as he was at sea when the child was conceived. The father, he asserts, is white. Moreover, Mary is now living in a state of "adultery, with divers persons," with the children suffering as innocent victims. Henry seeks a divorce, and requests that his wife be summoned to answer his complaint.

Result: No recorded result.

***

Petition 21283306
North Carolina Guilford County
1833 -1835

Abstract: Olivia Fields prays for a divorce from her husband, Emsly Fields, on the grounds of abuse, adultery, and selling her "at public auction like stock or slaves" while she was pregnant. **Result:** granted.

***

Petition 21283309
North Carolina Caswell County
February 18, 1833
Abstract: Andrew Whittington seeks a divorce from his wife Lucy Loftis Whittington for engaging in "criminal intercourse with both whites and mulattos" and for having "three illegitimate children, one of which is a coloured child."

Result: No recorded result

***

Petition 21283404
North Carolina, Person County
November 1834
Abstract: Married in 1826, Martha S. Evans seeks a divorce, charging her husband David Evans with abuse, adultery, and numerous assaults. In one incident, in 1832, when she discovered him "in the act of attempting to gratify his criminal desires on a negro woman" by force, Martha attempted to intervene. The petitioner's husband seized her, she recounts, "and inflicted on her such a beating that she was nearly helpless for a week." His only regret, he said the next morning, was that he had not killed her.

Result: No recorded result.

***

Petition 21283408
North Carolina, Wayne County
October 2, 1834

Abstract: Married about twenty-five years, Richard Jernigan seeks a divorce on the grounds that his wife "began to display evidence of a violent & outrageous temper," was addicted to "spirituous liquors," and was guilty of "libidinous intercourse with both black & white men." Indeed, he contracted a venereal disease from his wife.

Result: No recorded result.

***

Petition 21283905
North Carolina, Burke County
October 27, 1839

Abstract: After two years of marriage, Samuel Jimeson discovered that his wife Fatima was having "indiscriminate intercourse with other men," including a free man of color. Indeed, Samuel caught the two "in the criminal act and for that cause alone drove the defendant from his house and told her that he could not live with her in consequence of her prostitution." Samuel seeks a divorce.

Result: No recorded result.

***

Petition 21284004
North Carolina Burke County
November 19, 1840

Abstract: Married in 1799, Anne Wilson files for divorce after a two-year separation from her husband. She charges that William Wilson ordered "a negro woman whom he owned to inflict blows on her person," and kept another black woman as his mistress, "indulging himself in sexual intercourse" in the very bed "which she was in the habit of sleeping." She asks the court to award her certain property, including slaves.

Result: No recorded result

***

Petition 21284008
North Carolina Guilford County
1840
Abstract: William King charges that his "young & handsome" wife Mary was accepting "the embraces of other men." Standing by a window near their house, he overheard Mary and her sister planning a rendezvous. A few evenings later, he followed his wife to the house of her mother, "old lady Coley," where she said she was going for a visit. King discovered the mother was gone, while his wife and her sister entertained "two Mulatto fellows." Peering through a window, he saw Mary with her head on the lap of one of the men. He seeks a divorce. In her related answer, Mary denies her husband's allegations and charges that he left her alone many nights without any explanation, and that he subsequently moved in with a man of color and his three daughters.

Result: No recorded result.

***

Petition 21284206
North Carolina Rowan
1842 – 1843
Abstract: Emeline Adderton seeks a divorce. She states that her husband John Adderton is "altogether degraded & worthless." During the time they lived together, she informs the court, he was in the habit of having sex with his father's slaves; since their separation "his intercourse is of the same degraded character, & extends to those of his own colour also."

Result: granted.

***

Petition 21284303
North Carolina Lincoln County
1843

Abstract: When she discovered that her husband was "indulging in sexual intercourse with his own negro woman slave by the name of Polly," Elizabeth Clubb confronted David Clubb with the accusation. He "grew so violent & abusive," Elizabeth testifies, that she was forced to flee from their home. He had previously beaten her, she says, and had even permitted Polly to strike her, egging her on by saying that "she had not beaten your petitioner enough." After Elizabeth left, Polly gave birth to a baby boy. Elizabeth has no doubt about the boy's paternity. She asks for a divorce and alimony. In a related answer, David Clubb charges that his wife "communicated" to him a venereal disease and that he has discovered she was a common prostitute.

Result: No recorded result.

***

Petition 21284311*
North Carolina Guilford County
April 21, 1843 - 1845
Abstract: Laura Vanstore says that her husband James abandoned her "altogether, refused to let her live with him, maliciously keeps her out of his house, and drives her away." He sold his property, moved to another section of the county, and now lives with another woman. She asks for divorce and alimony. In his defense, James Vanstore said Laura gave birth to "a bastard child" before their marriage. Witnesses testified that the child's father was "Fultons Joe." The slave "took holt of her & commenced raising her Clothes," a witness to Laura's recounting the incident said, "then she replyed that you Know Joe such as this will not do he said he must have a little any how, Laura said that was about the time the Child was got."

Result: Granted.

Comments: *In plain speak, she is alleging that she was raped and impregnated by Joe. However, there seems to be a lack of follow-up action...was the alleged rape reported to* *the Sherriff, was Joe executed? It appears to me that the rape allegation is an attempt to deflect the allegation of sexual misconduct of which estranged husband* James Vanstore accuses her of.

***

Petition 21284313
North Carolina Stokes County
March 20, 1843
Abstract: After twenty-two years of marriage, Henry Shouse accuses his wife of having sex with one of his slaves, and giving birth to a child "of negro blood." He asks for a divorce.

Result: No recorded result.

***

Petition 21284505
North Carolina Craven County
March 2, 1845
Abstract: Four years after their marriage, Wesley Gray explains, his wife abandoned him "without the slightest cause or provocation." Now she keeps the "vilest company," and has "adulterous connection" with men of the "most unprincipled and abandoned characters, frequently boasting in public company of the great number of her conquests not only of white but of Coloured paramours."

Result: No recorded result.

***

Petition 21284508
North Carolina Randolph County
1845 - 1846
Abstract: Isaac Routh charges his wife with "adulterous intercourse with different men in the neighborhood," including the slave Daniel, owned by Aaron Jones. In addition, he asserts, she threatened to poison him, "actually Stabbed him & gave him a Severe wound," and boasted

about illicit affairs. She has since abandoned him and now lives with another man in another state.

Result: granted.

***

Petition 21284607
North Carolina Wake, County
July 25, 1846

Abstract: Sarah Jane Strickland accuses her husband of being "in habits of criminal intercourse with one of Mr. Ellington's negro women." She also states that he informed her on their wedding night "that he was affected with a certain venereal disease which he intended to give her and that he had made a bargain with a certain married man...to exchange wives every alternate night and that she would thus be compelled to sleep with this stranger every other night." He has abandoned her and left the county. She seeks a divorce.

Result: No recorded result *

***

Petition 21284610
North Carolina Ashe County
October 7, 1846

Abstract: Alfred White seeks a divorce. His wife, the former Jane Phipps, "eloped from his bead [sic] and board" with another man and made off to the state of Missouri. Prior to departing she was "seen with a Coloured man."

Result: No recorded result.

***

Petition 21284702
North Carolina Granville County
1847

Abstract: Amanda Walker accuses her husband of living "in constant unlawful intercourse with a certain negro woman belonging to his grand Father." She also accuses him of running off with the black woman and one or two other of his grandfather's slaves. He is also guilty of forgery. She asks for a divorce and alimony.

Result: No recorded result.

***

Petition 21284802
North Carolina Richmond County
July 8, 1848 - 1850
Abstract: After several years of marriage, to his "great grief, mortification and shame," Stephen Cole found out with anguish that his wife Mary "was delivered of a mulatto child." Upon investigation Cole discovered that Mary had probably committed adultery with a slave named Richmond who belonged to the estate of Daniel McDonald, deceased. He seeks a divorce. In her related answer to the charges, Mary Cole accuses her husband of domestic violence and drunkenness, and of forcing her to seek refuge in the kitchen where she slept among the slaves. She claims that she does not know what may have happened under such conditions. She also countercharges that her husband commits adultery with his own slave, Bet, who sleeps with them in the bed.

Result: Granted*

***

Petition 21285006
North Carolina Wayne County
April 2, 1850

Abstract: In the spring of 1847, John Sykes, along with many of his neighbors, volunteered for the Army, and left to fight in Mexico. In the months that followed he heard disquieting rumors that his wife was being unfaithful. When he returned in August of 1848 he discovered that she was "far advanced in a state of pregnancy." Even more humiliating, he said, she soon gave birth to a child "evidently begotten by some slave or free black person." Sykes seeks a divorce.

Result: granted.

***

Petition 21285022*
North Carolina, Wayne County 1850
Abstract: Married at age twelve to a thirty-year-old woman, Daniel Griffin, after twelve years of marriage, requests a divorce on the grounds that his wife was "guilty of adultery with diverse persons," including "a certain mulatto fellow named William Baker." In addition, she also gave birth to two bastard children. **Result:** Granted

***

Petition 21285023
North Carolina, Craven County
1850
Abstract: Slaveholder Harriet Foy asks for a divorce because of her husband's adultery "with various and sundry women." He has been guilty, she explains, "of living in general, habitual and indiscriminate adulterous intercourse with slaves and other abandoned women," particularly a slave woman named Hannah owned by a woman in Jones County. **Result:** No recorded result.

***

Petition 21285120
North Carolina New Hanover County
March 22, 1851-1854
Abstract: In 1824 or 1825, slave owner Hugh Lamb left his wife, who, he said, "was guilty of adulterous intercourse with a negro slave," and took his two daughters to live with his brother Isaac Lamb. As payment, he conveyed to his brother, in a trust estate, six slaves and his 350-acre farm, stipulating in return that he and his daughters would be "maintained and supported" from the hires and profits of the

slaves until he "departed this life." Then, "the whole of said property" would be conveyed to his daughters. In 1829, Hugh and his daughters moved in with his brother-in-law Edward Pigford, transferring the trust accordingly. Later, when his daughters marry, they receive several slaves, but in 1851 Hugh Lamb charges that he is no longer being "maintained and supported" by Pigford and sues his brother and brother-in-law, who nevertheless retains some of the slaves. Lamb is illiterate, and has "always possessed an understanding inferior to most of his fellow men."

Result: No recorded result.

***

Petition 21285205
North Carolina Person County
1852
Abstract: Within a few years after their marriage in 1842, Matilda Brooks charges, her husband became "very dissipated & drunken & spent a handsome estate which she brought him at marriage." She remained with him because of their two children. But when he became unfaithful and committed adultery with "diverse persons, but especially with a negro woman Lucy the property of William Baird," Matilda concluded she had no other choice but to ask for a divorce. She also sues for alimony and other relief "as her case may require." **Result:** granted.

***

Petition 21285319
North Carolina Craven County
September 10, 1853
 Abstract: After fifteen years of marriage, Mary Richardson seeks a divorce. She claims that Andrew Richardson is a drunkard, abuses and threatens her, and now lives in adultery with a free black woman.

Result: No recorded result.

***

Petition 21285320
North Carolina Granville County
August 26, 1853
Abstract: Eliza Ellis says that for more than twelve months her husband Philemon has been living with a slave woman named Effie in adultery. She seeks a divorce.

Result: No recorded result.

***

Petition 21285321
North Carolina Yadkin County
December 6, 1853
Abstract: Less than a year after their marriage, Rebecca Chamberlain was driven from her home by her husband, who subsequently took up with a free black woman. Rebecca has not lived with her husband since, although he has lived with several women, including Betsey Bunting, who bore him a child. Rebecca asks for a divorce, or, at the least, a "separation from bed & board" with a right to keep "all her subsequent acquisitions by gift or otherwise." **Result:** No recorded result.

***

Petition 21285428
North Carolina, Stanly County
March 6, 1854
Abstract: Andrew Troutman states that "his wife Catharine committed adultery by having criminal connection with one John Bennet, a free person of color." Indeed, he believes, she had "frequent casual intercourse" with Bennet over a period of time. Troutman seeks a divorce.

Result: granted.

***

Petition 21285505
North Carolina, Lincoln County
August 17, 1855- 1856

Abstract: Frances S. Courtney charges that her husband is "an habitual drunkard & spendthrift" who gratifies his "lustful disposition" with women "regardless either of the age or color of the objects of his amours." Indeed, he has had sex with white prostitutes, slaves, and free blacks. Recently, he abandoned her and moved to South Carolina, where he now lives with another woman. She asks for a divorce.

Result: granted.

***

Petition 21285529
North Carolina, Duplin County
1855 - 1856
Abstract: After a dozen years of marriage, Blany Williams discovers that his wife is probably having an affair with one of his slaves. He knows that she "indecently" exposed herself to the unnamed black man, and it seems difficult to believe that the man would have resisted her overtures. Indeed, on one occasion she was seen "on or near his bedside in the night time and in undress." Blany informs the court that his wife is an habitual drunkard who engages in unfeminine behavior, uses profane language, and exposes the lower and upper parts of her body to men visiting the house.

Result: granted

***

Petition 21285609
North Carolina Yadkin County
April 8, 1856
Abstract: Less than a year after he married in 1851, Kennedy M. Williams discovered that his wife Mary Eliza was sleeping with other men, including planter Samuel Speer and one of Speer's slaves, a man named Hand. Now, however, Williams has been declared non compos mentis and his guardian seeks a divorce in his behalf.

Result: No recorded result.

***

Petition 21285624
North Carolina, Guilford County
January 30, 1856 - 1858
Abstract: Free woman of color Jane Milton seeks a divorce from her husband Elisha Milton, who sold three of their children for a term of years to support his drinking habit. In addition, he beat her severely. He "fell upon her with a walking stick, on which he had a large Buckhorn handle or head, and abused her by beating her over the head & legs & shoulders in a most shameful & disgraceful manner." She was unable to walk for nearly a month. Now he has their only daughter and is living in adultery with another free woman of color. She seeks a divorce, and "all the rights & privileges of a feme sole -- according to the laws of this state." It is unclear whether Elisha Milton actually sold his sons as term slaves or whether he placed as indentured apprentices.

Result: granted.

Comments: *It would seem as if "freedom" itself, has inflicted Elisha with a cruel abusive mentality and drove him to excesses of vice.*

***

Petition 21285626
North Carolina, Guilford County
March 29, 1856
Abstract: Married only a few years, Mary Garrett, who brought a large dowry to the union, explains that following the birth of their first child, as her health declined, her husband became unkind, harsh, and unpleasant. Eventually he "abandoned her conjugal embraces" and took up with one of his slaves. In 1856, he left on a trip for the purpose of selling the slave and returned a few weeks later, much to his wife's surprise, with another mulatto female slave, "adorned in fine dress and Jewelry." Mary seeks alimony, and wishes to be allowed to manage her property. In addition to her

husband, she sues a number of other people, including her mother, Dejaina Doak, whose interests are tied in with Edward Garrett's assets.

Result: partially granted.

***

Petition 21285636
North Carolina, Franklin County
1856

Abstract: Married for more than two decades, Mary Ann Williams accuses her husband of drunkenness, violence, and adultery. Aside from his violent nature, she claims that he is having an extramarital affair with a free woman of color named Martha Fogg, who has given birth to a "white child." Compelled to leave her home, Mary Ann explains that her father recently died, leaving her property. She seeks to obtain custody of her father's estate, as well as a divorce and alimony. **Result:** No recorded result.

***

Petition 21285715
North Carolina Guilford County
1857 - 1859

Abstract: Robert Mitchell rejects the child delivered by his wife, the former Minerva Wallace of Guilford County, fifteen months after she abandoned him. He claims that she has committed adultery with several persons, including Ben, a slave owned by John King. He asks for a divorce.

Result: granted.

***

Petition 21285716
North Carolina, Guilford County
1857

Abstract: Married in 1854, Elisha Charles Dodson claims that his wife, the former Permelia Ann Brown, committed adultery. During different periods, he says, she lived with her mother, Betsey Brown, who managed a house of ill repute, and also with a free black man "who kept a house of the same bad character." Elisha seeks a divorce.

Result: No recorded result.

***

Petition 21285814
North Carolina, Randolph County
March 8, 1858
Abstract: Rhodias Riley seeks a divorce, charging that his wife left him six years before and that "she has kept up a promiscuous adulterous intercourse with divers other men particularly with Dave, a negro slave."

Result: No recorded result.

***

Petition 21285815
North Carolina Randolph County
September 29, 1858-1859
Abstract: When he was sixteen, Benjamin F. Millican married Elizabeth Holder, who was "much older," a "full grown woman." On the road hauling goods as a wagon man, Millican returned to find that his wife was having an affair with a young man in the neighborhood. Later, he said, she lived with a free family of color and was guilty of adultery with the son in the family, Frank Lytle. Benjamin Millican seeks a divorce.

Result: granted.

***

Petition 21285856
North Carolina, Guilford County
October 1858
Abstract: Henry Brady, a shopkeeper, informs the court that he was convicted of murdering John Knowles, his wife's alleged lover, and later pardoned He also informs the court

that he believes the last child born to his wife is not his, but John Knowles's child. In her answer, Jane Brady wife denies the charge of adultery, and accuses her husband of having illicit sex with a number of women, both black and white, forcing himself sexually on a girl of very tender years, and sexually forcing himself on his own sister. He also transmitted a venereal disease to his wife.

Result: No recorded result.

***

Petition 21286114
North Carolina, Randolph County
January 2, 1861
Abstract: Married in 1849, Nancy Jane Brooks seeks a divorce and alimony, charging that her husband, a teacher, is "a drunkard and spendthrift" who has slept with his hired slave and free black women. Indeed, she testifies, he kept up "shameless adulterous intercourse with divers negroes." In addition, on one occasion, he stripped her and whipped her mercilessly.

Result: No recorded result.

***

Petition 21286602
North Carolina, Wake County
October 3, 1866
Abstract: Returning home following Lee's surrender after fighting for four years in the Confederate Army, John H. Green discovered that his wife had had an affair with Jesse Hopson, a black man. In the summer of 1865, she gave birth to "a negro girl child." Green seeks a divorce.

Result: granted.

***

Petition 21286603
North Carolina Rowan County
April 20, 1866

Abstract: Sixty-nine-year-old James Bostian seeks a divorce from his wife Mary who "became the mother of a mulatto or negro child," and admitted that she had an affair with a black man. She has "a general bad character for virtue," the husband charges, "it being generally reported that she is unchaste as well with white men as negroes."

Result: No recorded result.

***

Petition 21286604
North Carolina Guilford County
July 18, 1866
Abstract: About 1854, Mary and John Hubbard, who were born free, obtained a marriage license from the Alamance County clerk of court and were married by a justice of the peace. After 1857, Mary testifies that John began to "ill-treat, beat, whip and abuse her;" he later became intimate with a woman named Emily, formerly the property of Tobias May and now a free woman. Mary claims that her husband continues to be intimate with the said Emily and cohabits with her. Mary asks for a divorce.

Result: No recorded result.

***

Petition 21286605
North Carolina Guilford County
September 1866

Abstract: After eight years of marriage, free born woman of color Zilphire Ann Goings charges her husband, who was also born free, with abuse, abandonment, and adultery. He mistreated and abused her, she explains, threatened to take her life, and lived in open adultery with Ruth Bass, a free woman of color. Meanwhile, Zilphire remained faithful to her vows of fidelity and chastity. She seeks a divorce.

Result: No recorded result.

***

Petition 21286609
North Carolina, Buncombe County
1866
Abstract: Mary L. Lytle petitions for divorce charging her husband with adultery, abusive behavior, and that he is "much inclined toward drunkenness." Moreover, he threatened to kill her, keeping a knife under his pillow and promising to "cut her throat." "This treatment," she asserts, "was habitual & as well when Sober as when he was drunk." She also accuses him of having had illicit intercourse with a "negro" or "mulatto" woman owned by his father. She claims that she "has good reason to believe that the same intercourse is kept up to this day." She seeks a divorce.

Result: No recorded result.

***

Petition 21383718
South Carolina Charleston District
June 27, 1837
Abstract: Eliza B. Prince seeks financial support from her husband, who has abandoned his family to live in "a state of vicious and illicit connection with a coloured woman" named Jemmima Jones. Eliza informs the court that she married John Prince twenty-six years ago and "faithfully and affectionately discharged all the duties of his wedded wife." She alleges that he began a liaison with Jemmima Jones thirteen or fourteen years ago and purchased her about ten years ago. Four years ago, he "entirely deserted" his wife and ten children, bought a house, and moved into it with Jemmima and her two children "in open contempt of the laws of God and man." Eliza avers that John "is an excellent book-keeper and that for several years he had earned a salary of about six or eight hundred dollars annually," but he spent most of his money on Jemmima, only occasionally giving his family small sums of money. She charges that John is about to leave the state with Jemmima and her children, depriving her and her children of their "just rights of

support and maintenance from his labour and property." The petitioner prays the court to issue writs of ne exeat and injunction to stop John from leaving the state and from disposing of Jemmima and her children. She also asks the court to compel her husband to support her and "his legitimate children." [The Master's Report and Recommendation in PAR #21383923 identifies Jemmima Jones as mulatto.]
Result: granted.

***

Petition 21484215
Tennessee, Smith County
September 5, 1842- August 1843
Abstract: Mary A. Harper seeks a divorce from her husband, Alfred Harper, and asks for "a reasonable suport out his estate." Mary claims that her husband began verbally and physically abusing her "about six weeks after said Marriage." In one violent episode, he seized her "by the hair of her head" and dragged her "over the house." He also began inviting "negroes to visit him at his own house" and, on a night in August 1842, he made an "arrangement to give a Super to the Negroes at 25 Cents a head & the use of his kitchen to dance in during the night & he remained with the Negroes dancing with them Most of the Night." Mary also accuses Alfred of committing "acts & deeds inconsistant with the matrimonial vow by conducting adultery with his sd. negroe woman Lacy." Informing the court that Alfred owns 119 acres of land, two slaves, and "stock of various kinds," she seeks an injunction, barring him from disposing of his estate until a final decree of the court. Alfred denies associating with "negroes ... on equal terms" in his answer. In a related petition, Mary Harper, recently divorced by court decree at August Term 1843, seeks custody of her infant child, who was born "whilst said Bill was pending in said court." She cites that her divorce from Alfred Harper was granted, but "no order was made in said decree as to who should have the custody of said child." She asks for custody

"of her said child free from the contact or disturbance of said Alfred."

Result: granted.

***

Petition 21485229
Tennessee, Washington County
June 22, 1852
Abstract: George Conley, a free man of color, seeks a divorce from his sixteen-year-old wife, Josephine, a free woman of color. Conley states that they were married in 1851 and that they lived together happily "for a short time". However, Josephine soon lost interest in the marriage and took an openly defiant step against her husband when, one day, she refused to make his dinner. When Conley "insisted to know of her what was the matter," she responded that she did not love him. She asserted "that there were men whose little fingers she cared more for than she did for complainants whole body." Josephine abandoned their home and since then "has been, almost perpetually keeping the company of other men, married and single, gallanting with them day and night, receiving and reciprocating love, in a most wanton and disgraceful manner." He charges that she has repeatedly committed adultery with a slave named Barney. Conley prays for a divorce "and that his relations to her may for all future time be as though the said marriage had never taken place." In her answer, Josephine states that she left Conley because he and his family physically and verbally abused her. She further accuses him of committing adultery "with a woman of color named Ester who belongs to one Jeremiah Gibson & who is old enough to be the mother of complainant."

Result: unknown.

***

Petition 21485444

Tennessee, Bradley County
August 1, 1854
Abstract: Eliza Graves seeks a divorce from her second husband, Simeon Graves, whom she married in 1844. She informs the court that "her happiness has been destroyed by the unnatural and adulterous practices of" her husband. She accuses Simeon of having an "improper intimacy" with his seventeen-year-old mulatto slave named Grace, who is "of quite seemly appearance." Grace "delivered a child, still or dead-born which was white," and whom Grace believes was "begotten by her said husband." Eliza has "ceased to recognize his rights as a husband since" and no longer cohabits with Simeon. She owns "in right of her first husband" four slaves, whom she fears Simeon intends to "transfer convey or encumber ... in some way." She asks the court to enjoin him from interfering with the slaves and to vest their title in her. She finally asks to be "restored to all the rights of a single woman." **Result:** partially granted.

***

Petition 21585501
Texas Brazoria
March26, 1855
Abstract: Sarah H. Black seeks a divorce from her husband, James E. Black. She reveals that Black has been "caught in the act of having illicit sexual intercourse" with two of his slaves, a mulatto woman named Susan and "a negro woman named Ann or Annie." When confronted, she asserts that her husband told her that "a damed good whipping or cowhiding would do her good, and he would give it to her unless she minded her own business." She further insists that her husband repeatedly called her a "god damned old bitch" and instructed the slaves not to obey her orders. The petitioner cites that slaves on the plantation had threatened her and had called her a liar, but the overseer informed her that he had been "given orders not to punish any of the servants at her request." She informs the court that her husband is the owner of a large plantation, which is community property,

and "some seventy or eighty slaves." She therefore prays for alimony and for custody of their children. **Result:** dismissed.

***

Petition 21681702
Virginia, Southampton County
December 16, 1817
Abstract: Through her next friend, Polly Gray seeks "some adequate support" from James Gray, her husband of thirty years. Charging that he is guilty of many offenses, the petitioner laments that he "has now for several years past pursued a system of conduct towards her cruel & tyrannical in the extreme;" that he "has for about six or seven years been continually in the habit of deserting the caresses of a fond & affectionate wife to whom he was bound by way ... of religion morality & law;" that he has "committed the worst open conjugal infidelities with prostitutes of the most abandoned order;" and that he "has taken to the very house in which they resided ... -- a wretch whose very colour is as sable as her crimes" and who "assails her with reproaches & insults which would be insufferable even from one more respectable." Forced to abandon their home, Polly notes that at the time of their marriage James was very poor and that she brought to the marriage a number of slaves, who "now with their increase" number sixteen or seventeen. Polly Gray prays that the court will secure to her a provision, "which security becomes ... necessary as the said James Gray is daily wasting and squandering on harlots those possessions which should be preserved for the comfort & support of your unfortunate oratrix." **Result:** unknown.

***

Petition 21683010
Virginia Lynchburg City
May 13, 1830

Abstract: Elizabeth Shomaker seeks a separation from her estranged husband, Zedekiah Shomaker, and "suitable maintainance for Life out of his estate." She represents that for a time she "lived happily with him performing in tenderness and affection the duties of a wife," but that Zedekiah soon began to treat her with cruelty. He had an "intolerable ill temper" and "connected himself illicitly with one of his own female slaves." She was thus compelled to leave his "Bed and Board" and now seeks alimony, arguing that he is in "good circumstances, worth two or more good tracts of Land Eight or more slaves and valuable Stock of all Kinds."

Result: unknown

***

Petition 21683340
Virginia Petersburg City
March 4, August 1833
Abstract: A. D. Williams, proprietress of a successful milliner's business in Petersburg, seeks a divorce from her husband, Henry Williams, "alias Hiram Whyte." She complains that about six months into their 1820 marriage, Henry "ceased to labour" and has "spent his time in idleness, frivolous amusements & the worst species of dissipation." He has indulged in "adulterous intercourse, with the lowest class of females & of all colours," and "frequently absented himself" from their home; on one occasion, he "started ostensibly to go to the Races near Richmond, but he was absent for four years." He has cruelly beat and abused her, gambled away her "hard earnings," and twice given her a venereal disease. Most recently, he has been living in "open adultery" with "one of the black population of this Town," a woman named Betsy Elbeck. Fearing that her savings will be "forcibly [w]rested from her by him," she asks for a divorce and for permission "to hold the property heretofore acquired by her own exertions, as a feme sole." Lengthy depositions

are rich with detail about Henry Williams "gambling & frolicking, drinking & carousing." **Result:** None recorded.

***

Petition 21684009
Virginia Campbell County
February 8, 1840
Abstract: Sarah H. Robinson seeks a divorce from her husband Samuel. She claims that her husband's conduct included "almost constant and habitual intoxication" and the "indolence and neglect of his family." Robinson further reveals that her husband exhibited a "tyrannical demeanor" toward her and her child and constantly threatened personal violence. Since their separation, Samuel has lived in adultery with a woman of "ill fame." In a related document, the jury found that Samuel has "notoriously lived in habits of illicit intercourse, with lewd women, both white and black, and had children by them."

Result: granted.

***

Petition 21684910
Virginia Petersburg City
March 1849 - November 1850
Abstract: Armstrong R. Blick petitions the court for a divorce from his wife Elizabeth. The petitioner charges "that the said Elizabeth about two or three years ago became disaffected & has since been guilty of adultery & living in common prostitution separate and apart from her husband." He therefore prays "that your Honor would by definitive sentence pronounce and decree the marriage to be null & void, pursuant to the Act of Assembly March 18 1848." In his deposition, R. C. Trayler informed the court that he saw Elizabeth "upon several occasion going into houses of ill fame, and I have seen her repeatedly in houses kept for that purpose by negroes -- that is for purposes of prostitution."

Result: granted.

***

Petition 21685001
Virginia Albemarle County
February 1850 – October 18, 1853
Abstract: Hillary Wood seeks a divorce from his wife Ruthy, claiming that she is "guilty of adultery with divers persons." The petitioner further asserts that his wife "deserted him and has for the last two years been living in a state of open prostitution with a black & white." Being "greatly aggrieved & mortified by this conduct" of his wife, Wood seeks "a severance of the ties which bind him to his said wife."

Result: granted.

***

Petition 21685230
Virginia, Petersburg City
March-May 1852
Abstract: Watkins Jones, a free person of color, asks for a divorce from his wife, Arena. Jones represents that "in the year 1845 the said Arena voluntarily deserted your orator, without any just cause of complaint against him, and commenced an adulterous connection with a certain Gilbert Bailey, and she has ever since that time up to the present hour lived a life of the most shameless depravity." The petitioner contends that his wife "is now living with a certain Thomas Parham, a free man of colour in this city." Citing that he "has not cohabited with her since such acts of adultery were committed, he is entitled to a divorce from the bond of matrimony." The petitioner also prays that "he be not required to make any provision for the future support of his said wife."

Result: granted.

***

Petition 21685327
Virginia, Franklin County
July19, 1853 - October, 1855

Abstract: Fifty-nine-year-old Milly Perdue seeks a divorce from Isaiah Perdue, whom she married when she was quite young and to whom she "has born ... a large family of children." Perdue maintains that for many years they lived together in peace and happiness, working "together side by side in the same field," and "that the property of which he is now possessed was procured to a considerable extent by the joint labour of your oratrix and her husband." The petitioner laments, however, that his conduct toward her changed as "she became advanced in years." She cites that "he has of late years been insufferably abusive and violent in his treatment to her." She recounts that he has "beaten her with his fists sticks and wagon whips in a most cruel and unfealing manner and has repeatedly threatened to kill her and do other severe bodily injury to her." In addition, he "frequently had illicit intercourse with a negro woman belonging to him and residing on the same place with your oratrix by whom he has had several children." Admitting that she has fled to the home of "a friend and relation," the petitioner prays for a divorce and sufficient "provision for her support."

Result: granted.

***

Petition 21685420
Virginia Petersburg City
March-May 1854
Abstract: Joseph W. Magee seeks a divorce from his wife Margaret, charging that Margaret has been "too intimate with other men and was guilty of adultery with them." Joseph continues by stating that Margaret has "visited houses of ill fame, known brothels, and has also been on terms of great intimacy with common strumpets." Joseph also seeks custody of five-year-old Henry James and eighteen-month-old Joseph. Depositions reveal that Margaret committed adultery at the house of Eliza Gallee, a free woman of color.
Result: granted.

***

Petition 21685526
Virginia Albemarle County
April 7, 1855 – May 26, 1856
Abstract: Susan A. Gully seeks a divorce from her husband William. Reporting that they lived happily together "for some eight or ten years," Gully "regrets to be compelled to say that the conduct of her husband has been for several passed very different from what it should be ... [that] she had reason to suspect his fidelity to the marriage vow." She laments that she later discovered that he "applied most of his wages to the support of a free negro woman" and that "finally he abandoned your oratrix and her four children left the town of Charlottesville ... in company with the negro woman above refered to, and has never returned." Susan admits "that it is true he has made some advances towards a reconciliation but your oratrix believes these overtures were never made in good faith, and she fears if she were to receive him again as her husband, he would not abandon his vicious practices." Citing "that the children are getting old enough to be of some service," Susan fears William "may demand their custody." In addition to "a divorce from the bond of matrimony," she asks that she be given custody of her children and that William provide for their support.

Result: granted.

***

Petition 21685605
Virginia Mecklenburg County
September 9, 1856 - March14, 1857
Abstract: Lucy P. Burwell seeks a divorce from her husband John. She states that her marriage was happy for many years and that she bore him eight children. She reveals, however, that his treatment towards her and her children has "sadly changed." Lucy attributes this change to his steadily growing "habits of intemperance," attesting that John is "now rarely free from the influence of intoxicating drinks." She admits "with humiliation ... that he has contracted an

improper and disreputable intimacy with one of his own female slaves, which she believes has existed for several years." Lucy confesses that she was horrified when John announced in the presence of their children "that he would not share her bed that night, but would occupy a different room" with "the female slave aforesaid, who remained in the room with him during the night." Lucy asserts that "this girl has within a few years past been the mother of two children the offspring of a white father," and she believes that John fathered the children. Lucy also claims that John violently beat her; on one occasion he "rudely pressed her up against the wall, choked her, and then struck her violently on each side of her face." Fleeing to the kitchen, Lucy recounts that John "ordered his slaves to pursue her," and she asserts that "a boy Enoch, actually offered to lay his hands on her, but was deterred by her resistance." She argues that she is "virtually a prisoner at home," citing that John once paid five slaves five dollars to prevent her leaving. The petitioner prays for a divorce, custody of her four younger children and a determination "in relation to the interest of your oratrix in her husband's estate," which includes "some 30 slaves or more" and land. **Result:** partially granted.

***

Petition 21685907
Virginia Petersburg City
October 1859
Abstract: John Taylor, a free man of color, seeks a divorce from his wife, Nancy Taylor, a free woman of color. He recounts that they were married in 1855 and "lived together in great harmony untill your Orator returning home late at night found her in bed with another man." Citing "his sense of duty to himself," Taylor admits that he "has been compelled to abandone her as his wife and since that time the said Nancy has been living in open adultery." The petitioner therefore prays "that the marriage aforesaid celebrated heretofore between your Orator and the said Nancy may be wholly annulled and declared void."

Result: unknown.

***

Petition 21685915
Virginia Halifax County
April14, 1859
Abstract: Rebecca A. Spragins seeks a divorce from her husband, Dr. Leonidas D. Spragins. Citing that they were married "on the 2nd day of March 1858," Rebecca charges that his conduct "was such that she was compelled to leave him that his treatment to her was cruel and that she was under great apprehension of bodily hurt indeed she charges that her life was in great danger." She further avows that her husband "was guilty of Adultery with one of his own slaves a negro girl named Lucy Ann" and that "in fact the said Spragins boasted of his illicit intercourse with others & other negro women." The petitioner notes that the said Spragins "is the owner in fee simple of a valuable tract of land," comprised of some 900 acres and worth "at least ten thousand Dollars;" he also owns 18 slaves. Fearful that he "will convert his property into money & remove the proceeds out of the Commonwealth" and that he will "take off his negroes & sell them," the petitioner prays "the court decree unto your oratrix a Divorce from the Bond of Matrimony from the said Spragins and make such division of the estate of the said Spragins as may [be] just & proper." She further requests that the sheriff "be required to take possession of the slaves aforesaid & hire them out till the further order of the Court."

Result: granted

***

Petition 21686007
Virginia Petersburg City
April 2, - May1860
Abstract: Elizabeth Armistead "free woman wife of Joseph Armistead" seeks a divorce from her husband, a free man of

color. The petitioner laments that the said Joseph "has frequently been insufferably abusive to her and drove her away from his house, until to protect herself from his violence and mal treatment she was compelled to fly his residence and seek refuge in the house of her mother Nancy Walden." Armistead further reveals that her husband has cohabited with another woman, living "with her in open adultery, having his washing done by her and sleeping with her contrary to his marriage vows." Noting that "the only property owned by your oratrix is one moiety of a lot and tenement ... which will become mine at the death of my Mother," the petitioner prays that she "may be entirely divorced and the marriage be dissolved" and that her said real property "will not be subject to his demands or use, or any way liable to his debts."

Result: granted.

***

Petition 21686010
Virginia Petersburg City
August 30-September 1860
Abstract: Bryant Day, a free man of color, seeks a separation from "his wife a free woman of Colour named Mary Jane." Bryant asserts that "he has been kind, affectionate and faithful ... and that he has done all that a man of his station and Position in life can do to merit a return of affection, duty and faithfulness." Confessing that the said Mary Jane "has been unkind, devoid of affection," the petitioner reveals that his wife is "frequently drunk and living in most wanton violation of every marriage requirement, living in constant and open adultery." Day prays "that your Honor would decree a Separation between them from the Bond of Marriage," as "he has been "wofully disappointed" in his marriage. **Result:** dismissed.

***

Petition 21686012

Virginia Lynchburg City
May - June 1860
Abstract: William H. Cochran seeks a divorce from his wife, Lucinda Cochran. The plaintiff accuses his wife of "having fallen into habits of intemperance," and he admits that she "has been for months past, living separate and apart from your Orator; changing her residence from one house of ill-fame to another in the city or it's vicinity, and living in undisguised habits of adultery and lewd intercourse." Being "advised that he is entitled to a divorce from the bond of matrimony with the said Lucinda," the petitioner prays "for a decree for a divorce ... without being compelled to provide for her support; also that the custody of his said children be secured to him; that said Lucinda Cochran be compelled to resume her maiden name, and barred forever from all rights of distribution and dower in your Orator's estate." A deposition reveals that Lucinda is residing in a house "occupied by free negroes, & of course has such reputation, that no decent white woman would make it a place of visitation or abode."
Result: granted.

***

Petition 11282708
North Carolina Wayne County
December 11, 1827
Abstract: Ann Borden asks that the divorce petition soon to be filed by her husband Jesse be rejected. She relates that she left Jesse four months after their marriage because of "ill treatment" and "many desperate threats made by said Borden against her life." She also admits that a month before her marriage she "had the misfortune to have a child born of which Jesse Borden was not the father"; Ann argues, however, that she never tried to conceal the fact that the child was not his and that he never voiced any qualms about rearing another man's child. The petitioner further asserts that attempting to pass the child off as his "would have been

unavailing as the child would unavoidably have shown for itself." Ann therefore prays "that the Legislature of North Carolina will preserve inviolate the ties of matrimony that exist between your Petitioner and Jesse Borden." A summary of Jesse's petition reveals that he thought the child was his because "previous to his marriage he had been in habits of illicit intercourse with her during which time she became pregnant"; that Jesse "did believe in the early infancy of the child that it was his and being desirous of making her what reperation was in his power for the loss of her virtue he intermarried with her immediately after the birth of the child"; and that he exclaimed "to his mortification and astonishment" said infant "to be a mulatto child the fruits of [a] negro."

Result: rejected.

***

Petition 11282712
North Carolina New Hanover County
November 29, 1827
Abstract: Jonathan Bryan seeks a divorce from his wife Ann Jane Anders, who not only attempted to kill him but also incited "an Insurrection" among his slaves. Bryan reports that the said Ann Jane attempted to poison him more than once; that she failed to nurse him when he "was Confined with the Billious fever So that his life was despaired of"; that she "has laid voiolent hands on his person twice;" that she has "treated with Cruelty the Seven Children he has had by a decent and former wife"; that she "took medicine" to induce a miscarriage when she returned from being absent "for the Space of eleven months dureing which time She got herself with Child;" and that he "has not seen the Said Ann Jane and has been for Som time past and at this time She is aliveing in a Negro house With Negros." He therefore prays that the legislature will "interpose and pass a Law Divorcing him from this wife Ann Jane."

Result: House: read, referred; report unfavorable.

***

Petition 11384706
South Carolina Barnwell District/Parish
November 1847
Abstract: Marmaduke Jones requests a divorce or annulment of his marriage to Ann Ross Jones on the grounds that she gave birth to a "mulatto" child. Marmaduke maintains that the couple married on 13 January 1847 and that on 24 August 1847 his wife "was brought to bed, and then and there delivered of a mulatto child." The petitioner, "well knowing (under the circumstances above set forth) that it is impossible for [him] to live with the said Ann, as husband and wife," therefore prays that he "may be released from the said Ann and that [he] and the said Ann may stand in the same relation to Each other, as though they never had been married."

Result: No recorded result.

***

Petition 11481926
Tennessee Davidson County
September 29, 1819
Abstract: Norfleet Perry of Davidson County seeks a divorce from his wife, Rachael, because she was "delivered of a mulatto child." Producing "affidavits of several most respectable persons acquainted with the fact of marriage," Perry prays "your Honorable body to interpose your power in his behalf by dissolving the bonds of matrimony between your petitioner, and the said Rachael Perry." The petitioner "is advised" that the circuit courts do not have the authority to decree divorces.

Results: referred to select committee.

Repository: Tennessee State Library and Archives, Nashville, Tennessee

Legislative Petitions; Document Number 47-1819-1-6; Microfilm Reel #6.

***

Petition 10185701
Alabama Coffee County
December 7, 1857
Abstract: Seventy-seven white citizens of Coffee County seeks residency status for Narcissa Daniel, a "free colored girl about seventeen years of age," who had come to Alabama from Georgia with Allen Daniel, "a highly Respectable" citizen. Narcissa, the petitioners claim, was the "offspring of a white woman of high family." Mrs. Daniel was her best friend and Narcissa would prefer a "state of bondage to that of separation."

Result: denied.

***

Petition 11000017
Mississippi
Date Not Specified
Abstract: John Baptiste Nicaisse purchased his two-year-old daughter, Izabella, in 1806 at the Bay of St. Louis, which was then under Spanish rule. The bill of sale stipulated that Nicaisse should legally emancipate the child "before the command't at mobile." Before Nicaisse could do so, however, the area became part of the

United States. He now seeks to free her through the Mississippi legislature.

Result: No recorded result.

***

Petition 11000024
Jefferson County
Date Not Specified
Abstract: A dozen residents of Jefferson County verify that Malachi Hagins, a widower, was married to a white woman.

The couple had ten children. On all occasions Hagins conducted himself "with great propriety" as an "honest and upright man." He had long been a member of the Baptist church. The petitioners ask the legislature to extend to Hagins and his children the right to sue and be sued and "all the rights privileges and immunities of a free white persons of this state." A related petition reveals that Malachi Hagins was born of free parents and that his grandmother was a white woman.

Result: No recorded result.

***

Petition 11082101
Mississippi Hancock County
September 8, 1821
Abstract: About 1818, John Morin purchased his eighteen-month-old slave daughter, described as a "quartroon" girl named Adele. Morin then went to the justice of the peace in Hancock County and procured an "act of emancipation." A short time later Morin died. His mother, Louise Favre, discovered that the act was not valid. She asks the legislature for an act of emancipation to free Adele. Favre states that she has six children by her former husband, Peter Morin, and that one of them is threatening to keep Adele in bondage. The mother laments that she is growing old and wants to respect her son's wish before she dies.

Result: No recorded result.

***

Petition 11279208
North Carolina Pasquotank County
December 1, 1792
Abstract: Jeremiah Symons represents that he is "in possession of three that are mixed blood David Joan & Abby and to me Slaves." He therefore prays, "from Contientious principles," that "an Act may be passed as may secure to them the Free injoyment of their Liberty."

Result: No recorded result.

***

Petition 11279308
North Carolina Bladen County
December 13, 1793
Abstract: John Hall represents that he "is possessed in his own right of a certain female slave of mixed Blood about the age of five years called Judith." He further explains that said child "is the Offspring of a Gentleman who is lately deceased to which Gentleman on his Death bed, your petioner entered into a solemn promise" that he "would endeavour to procure the manumition and freedom of the said female slave." Hall, in pursuance of his "sacred promise," prays "that by an Act of this General Assembly the said female slave may be emancipated & set free by the name of Judith Phillips."

Result: House, Senate: read, referred.

***

Petition 11280102
North Carolina Randolph County
December 8, 1801
Abstract: Eighteen residents of Randolph County report that the late John Bagnel "left two Mulato [female] Children whose mother is also dead & left no will in writing altho possessed of some personal property." The petitioners aver that they are "fully satisfied that he own'd sd. children to be his & wish'd them to injoy the little property he was possessed of." They therefore pray that a law be passed "as may Entitle them to freedom & to inherit what little property may be found." They further "desire their Names to be Established Sarah Bagnell & Hannah Bagnell."

Result: Senate, House: read, referred.

***

Petition 11280516
North Carolina Edgecombe County
December 9, 1805

Abstract: Winny Manning confesses that her husband Eli "is absolutely impotent & by nature rendered a useless man as a husband." She admits that as "unpleasant as that may appear to a young & healthy woman" it is "but trifling" compared to his suspicions of her entertaining "illicit connection with every man, both white & black that may have seen her," which at times has resulted in a "certain danger of her life." Winny therefore asks that an act be passed divorcing her "from the said Eli Manning." Eli Manning, "on his part," states that "the happy ends for which matrimony was ordained has been frustrated & rendered a fruitfull sorce of the most unpleasant reflections and that reconciliation will never take place." He therefore "begs leave most freely & sincerely to join his sd Wife Winny in praying your honorable body to relieve your truly suffering Petitioners by granting them a divorce."

Result: rejected.

***

Petition 11280902
North Carolina Ashe County
November 27, 1809
Abstract: Alexander Smith seeks a divorce from his wife Sarah Dickson Smith. He states that he married Sarah in 1784 and that they lived together for many years "in domestic peace and pleasure," raising a family of five girls. Smith confides, however, that Sarah "became base in her conduct" and in 1808 "she went off with a Mullatoe man nearly as Black as an Negro and has lived without the Bounds of this State with said man of mixt collur ever since." The petitioner prays that he be divorced from his wife Sarah and that she be forever prevented "in Law or in Equity to Claim any right Title or interest to any part of your Petitioner's Estate or property real or personal."

Result: granted.

***

Petition 11280905

North Carolina Wilkes County
December 18, 1809
Abstract: John P. Waters, "a very poor man," admits that he "became attached" to Elisabeth Culms, a woman of color, who moved into his house in 1795; fourteen years later, he and the said Elisabeth have "six fine children." He further relates that he "did Intend to make her his lawfull wife but being informed that such a connection would be Illegal it was from time to time defered to the present day." Waters states, however, that "envy and Malice has at last siezed on the heart of a neighbor who gave our Solisitor Information of my unfortunate Situation and manner of living," whereby he and Elisabeth were indicted and fined twenty-five pounds apiece "for living together in an unlawfull manner." The petitioner prays that the said fines may be remitted or that he be granted "other relief as you in your wisdom may think fit."

Result: rejected.

COMMENTS: Procrastination is the thief of time! –EDWARD YOUNG-Night thoughts.

***

Deed Book E: 619
Laurens & Newberry Counties, SC
1785-1827

January 13, 1803, Deed of Emancipation, Thomas Wadsworth Esquire, late of Charleston and State of South Carolina, merchant, deceased, by his last will and testament dated at Charleston 14 September 1799, set free Archibald commonly called Archibald Rox, a mulatto boy about 9 years of age reputed to be the son of a white woman and born free, who formed part of the testators family and was bound to him for a term of years..Signed William Turpin, Benj. Cudsworth, John T. Elsworth, P. Butler, Junr. Recorded 1 March 1802. Fredk. Nance, R.M.C.

COMMENTS: The back-story of many early American families and therein lays a mystery or perhaps, more of an aberrant narrative that intertwines with so many lives of Southern Black and White Americans that it is often difficult to plot their separate interests.

***

Petition 11382125
South Carolina Charleston District/Parish 1821
Abstract: Phillipe Stanislaus Noisette, "Botanist of Charleston," reveals that he "has, under peculiar circumstances become the Father of Six children begotten upon his faithful Slave named Celestine." Noisette admits that "it has been the intention of your petitioner for many years past by complying with the then existing Laws of the State, to emancipate the said Celestine and such of her children as were then alive, but unfortunately, he procrastinated the measure until after the passage of the late Law upon this subject." The petitioner therefore prays that his "peculiarly unfortunate" situation be given consideration as he fears "should any accident befal him, his own children and their mother, who by her exemplary conduct is well entitled to her freedom, would probably all become the slaves of another."

Result: No recorded result.

COMMENTS: *It is our daily duty to consider that in all circumstances of life, pleasurable, painful, or otherwise, the conduct of every human being affects more or less, the happiness of others, especially of those in the same house; and that, as life is made up, for the most part, not of great occasions, but of small everyday moments, it is the giving to those moments their greatest amount of peace, pleasantness, and security, that contributes most to the sum of human good. Be peaceable. Be cheerful. Be true. - LEIGH HUNT.*

***

Petition 11678001
Virginia Richmond City

November 11, 1780

Abstract: Benjamin Bilberry, a free person of color, traded land for his wife Kate, a slave held by Abraham Cowley. Bilberry laments, however, that "this purchase instead of liberating his said wife & freeing her perpetually from the Shackles of Bondage has only changed her master." He acknowledges that to even "his uncultivated Mind it is irksome to know that he himself, by the Laws of this, now independant Common Wealth, is forced to hold his own Wife in a Slavish Bondage without the power of making her as free as himself." The petitioner therefore prays that "no policy may restrict your Honor from suffering him to enjoy the sweet reflection of having spent the whole labours of his Life in bestowing freedom on one equal by nature ... to himself & whom he has chosen to be the partner of his worldly Cares."

Result: granted.

COMMENTS: *His "uncultivated mind" knew the right thing to do. His romantic feelings and commitment to his wife were not entirely illusory. His love for her gave him a real sense of possibilities of how their lives might be if they were able to actualize their highest potential for loving each other as husband and wife, not slave to master. No doubt his romantic fantasies of her, was in essence the intuition about their possible future life together, that created a state of heightened vision - a sense of common purpose for being together. Enslavement of the body is compulsory; enslavement of the heart is voluntary.*

***

From these petitions, you can determine that most free-Black and mulatto had advantages denied to slaves. They also faced certain challenges not faced by slaves and the advantages and the challenges are apparent in some of these petitions. What I find myself doing when I read these petitions, is asking myself, "What would I have done in that situation, could I have endured, prevailed or made a difference?" After all, interracial relations were from the outset an arena for critical and historical conflicts between the races, yet the contradiction between institutionalized behavior and what was common practice was recorded in these petitions. Were our ancestors hypocrites, preaching against forbidden fruits while harvesting the bounty thereof?

These petitions tell fascinating, humorous, and heartbreaking life stories, particularly involving Mulattos. Their fair complexions sometimes mitigated the disadvantages of race. However, in spite of their white ancestry, and in some cases could not be visibly distinguished from whites, as some of these petitions attest, they nevertheless, were identified first and foremost with their African kinfolk. I believe, It was the cultural rather than biological experience of race that shaped America's racial consciousness and caused it to be "**Color Struck!**" and enact the following laws:

State	First law passed	Law repealed	Races banned from marrying whites	Note
Arizona	1865	1962	Blacks, Asians, Filipinos, Indians	Filipinos ("Malays") and Indians ("Hindus") added to list of "races" in 1931
California	1850	1948	Blacks, Asians, Filipinos	Anti-miscegenation law overturned by state judiciary in Supreme Court of California case *Perez v. Sharp*
Colorado	1864	1957	Blacks	
Idaho	1864	1959	Blacks, Native Americans,	

State				
Indiana	1818	1965	Asians Blacks	
Maryland	1692	1967	Blacks, Filipinos	Repealed its law in response to the start of the *Loving v. Virginia* case
Montana	1909	1953	Blacks, Asians	
Nebraska	1855	1963	Blacks, Asians	
Nevada	1861	1959	Blacks, Native Americans, Asians, Filipinos	
North Dakota	1909	1955	Blacks	
Oregon	1862	1951	Blacks, Native Americans, Asians, Native Hawaiians	
South Dakota	1909	1957	Blacks, Asians, Filipinos	
Utah	1852	1963	Blacks, Asians, Filipinos	
Wyoming	1913	1965	Blacks, Asians, Filipinos	

Anti-miscegenation laws overturned on 12 June 1967 by *Loving v. Virginia*

State	First law passed	Races banned from marrying whites	Note
Alabama	1822	Blacks	Repealed during Reconstruction, law later reinstated
Arkansas	1838	Blacks	Repealed during Reconstruction, law later reinstated
Delaware	1721	Blacks	
Florida	1832	Blacks	Repealed during Reconstruction, law later reinstated
Georgia	1750	All non-whites	
Kentucky	1792	Blacks	
Louisiana	1724	Blacks	Repealed during Reconstruction, law later reinstated
Mississippi	1822	Blacks, Asians	Repealed during Reconstruction, law later reinstated
Missouri	1835	Blacks, Asians	
North Carolina	1715	Blacks, Native Americans	
Oklahoma	1897	Blacks	
South Carolina	1717	All non-whites	Repealed during Reconstruction, law later reinstated
Tennessee	1741	Blacks, Native Americans	
Texas	1837	Blacks, Filipinos	
Virginia	1691	All non-whites	Previous anti-

miscegenation law
made more severe by
<u>Racial Integrity Act of
1924</u>

West
Virginia   1863   Blacks

The Virginia miscegenation law in 1691 specified;

"And for prevention of that abominable mixture and spurious issue which hereafter may encrease in this dominion, as well by negroes, mulattoes, and Indians intermarrying with English, or other white women, as by their unlawfull accompanying with one another, *Be it enacted by the authoritie aforesaid, and it is hereby enacted,* that for the time to come, whatsoever English or other white man or woman being free shall intermarry with a negroe, mulatto, or Indian man or woman bond or free shall within three months after such marriage be banished and removed from this dominion forever. . . ."

Another section of the law closed the loophole created by the 1662 birthright law, which mandated that children born of a free white mother and Negro father were technically free. This amendment stated that a free white woman who had a bastard child by a Negro or mulatto man had to pay fifteen pounds sterling within one month of the birth. If she could not pay, she would become an indentured servant for five years. Whether or not the fine was paid, however, the child would be bound in service for thirty years.

The laws that restricted slaves or indentured servants generally addressed the owners and penalized them for breaking the law. Laws governing slaves allowed masters to beat or kill them under certain circumstances. Nor could they go to court to seek redress. A person of color was not permitted to testify against a white Christian, as illustrated by the 1717 Maryland law:

"Be it Therefore Enacted, *by the right honourable the Lord Proprietary, by and with the advice and consent of his Lordship's Governor, and the Upper and Lower Houses of Assembly, and by the authority of the same,* That from and after the end of this present session of assembly, no Negro or mulatto slave, free Negro, or mulatto born of a white woman, during his time of *servitude by law,* or any Indian slave, or free Indian natives, of this or the neighbouring provinces, be admitted and received as good and valid evidence in law, in any matter or thing whatsoever depending before any court of record, or before any magistrate within this province, wherein any christian white person is concerned."

Reviewing these historical records makes it clear that economic class and gender, as well as heritage and physical appearance, played an integral part in shaping one's racial identity, and this leads us into the next collection of Petitions titled, "Passing for White." After reading the previous petitions, you may wonder as I have, how many of the "So Called white women were in fact "Mulattos." Innocent of adultery, but guilty of passing for white, only to be found out by the complexions of their children, willfully suffering the accusation of adultery rather than own up to that "One Drop" of Black-Blood in their veins. Being accused of adultery, she could live down after many years, but having "One-Drop" of black blood in the gene pool, poisoned the whole well for her entire family.

"The **one-drop rule** is a historical colloquial term in the United States for the social classification as black, for individuals with any African ancestry; meaning any person with "one drop of black blood" was considered black. The principle was an example of hypodescent, the automatic assignment of children of a mixed union between different socioeconomic or ethnic groups to the group with the lower status. The one-drop rule was not adopted as law until the twentieth century: first in Tennessee in 1910 and in Virginia under the Racial Integrity Act of 1924 (following the passage of similar laws in numerous other states).

Despite the strictures of slavery, in the antebellum years, free people of mixed race could have up to one-eighth or one-quarter African ancestry (depending on the state) and be considered legally white. More were absorbed into the majority culture based simply on appearance, associations and carrying out community responsibilities. These and community acceptance were more important factors if a person's racial status were questioned, not his or her documented ancestry. The mobility of the society meant that many people did not have documentation about their ancestors. Thomas Jefferson's four surviving "natural" children by his mixed-race slave Sally Hemings were seven-eighths European in ancestry and thus legally white although they were born into slavery. Three of the four entered white society as adults, two married white persons, and all their descendants identified as white. Many of later generations of his mixed-race descendants also entered white society, according to their appearance."

(Wikipedia, the free encyclopedia)

The following statement was adopted by the Executive Board of the American Anthropological Association, acting on a draft prepared by a committee of representative American anthropologists. It does not reflect a consensus of all members of the AAA, as individuals vary in their approaches to the study of "race." We believe that it represents generally the contemporary thinking and scholarly positions of a majority of anthropologists.

In the United States both scholars and the general public have been conditioned to viewing human races as natural and separate divisions within the human species based on visible physical differences. With the vast expansion of scientific knowledge in this century, however, it has become clear that human populations are not unambiguous, clearly demarcated, biologically distinct groups. Evidence from the analysis of genetics (e.g., DNA) indicates that most physical variation, about 94%, lies *within* so-called racial groups. Conventional geographic "racial" groupings differ from one another only in about 6% of their genes. This means that there is greater variation within "racial" groups than between them. In neighboring populations there is much overlapping of genes and their phenotypic (physical) expressions. Throughout history whenever different groups have come into contact, they have interbred. The continued sharing of genetic materials has maintained all of humankind as a single species.

Physical variations in any given trait tend to occur gradually rather than abruptly over geographic areas. And because physical traits are inherited independently of one another, knowing the range of one trait does not predict the presence of others. For example, skin color varies largely from light in the temperate areas in the north to dark in the tropical areas in the south; its intensity is not related to nose shape or hair texture. Dark skin may be associated with frizzy or kinky hair or curly or wavy or straight hair, all of which are found among different indigenous peoples in tropical regions. These facts render any attempt to establish lines of division among biological populations both arbitrary and subjective.

Historical research has shown that the idea of "race" has always carried more meanings than mere physical differences; indeed, physical variations in the human species have no meaning except the social ones that humans put on them. Today scholars in many fields argue that "race" as it is understood in the United States of America was a social mechanism invented during the 18th century to refer to those populations brought together in colonial America: the English and other European settlers, the conquered Indian peoples, and those peoples of Africa brought in to provide slave labor.

From its inception, this modern concept of "race" was modeled after an ancient theorem of the Great Chain of

Being, which posited natural categories on a hierarchy established by God or nature. Thus "race" was a mode of classification linked specifically to peoples in the colonial situation. It subsumed a growing ideology of inequality devised to rationalize European attitudes and treatment of the conquered and enslaved peoples. Proponents of slavery in particular during the 19th century used "race" to justify the retention of slavery. The ideology magnified the differences among Europeans, Africans, and Indians, established a rigid hierarchy of socially exclusive categories underscored and bolstered unequal rank and status differences, and provided the rationalization that the inequality was natural or God-given. The different physical traits of African-Americans and Indians became markers or symbols of their status differences.

As they were constructing US society, leaders among European-Americans fabricated the cultural/behavioral characteristics associated with each "race," linking superior traits with Europeans and negative and inferior ones to blacks and Indians. Numerous arbitrary and fictitious beliefs about the different peoples were institutionalized and deeply embedded in American thought.

Early in the 19th century the growing fields of science began to reflect the public consciousness about human differences. Differences among the "racial" categories were projected to their greatest extreme when the argument was posed that Africans, Indians, and Europeans were separate species, with Africans the least human and closer taxonomically to apes.

Ultimately "race" as an ideology about human differences was subsequently spread to other areas of the world. It became a strategy for dividing, ranking, and controlling colonized people used by colonial powers everywhere. But it was not limited to the colonial situation. In the latter part of the 19th century it was employed by Europeans to rank one another and to justify social, economic, and political inequalities among their peoples. During World War II, the

Nazis under Adolf Hitler enjoined the expanded ideology of "race" and "racial" differences and took them to a logical end: the extermination of 11 million people of "inferior races" (e.g., Jews, Gypsies, Africans, homosexuals, and so forth) and other unspeakable brutalities of the Holocaust.

"Race" thus evolved as a worldview, a body of prejudgments that distorts our ideas about human differences and group behavior. Racial beliefs constitute myths about the diversity in the human species and about the abilities and behavior of people homogenized into "racial" categories. The myths fused behavior and physical features together in the public mind, impeding our comprehension of both biological variations and cultural behavior, implying that both are genetically determined. Racial myths bear no relationship to the reality of human capabilities or behavior. Scientists today find that reliance on such folk beliefs about human differences in research has led to countless errors.

At the end of the 20th century, we now understand that human cultural behavior is learned, conditioned into infants beginning at birth, and always subject to modification. No human is born with a built-in culture or language. Our temperaments, dispositions, and personalities, regardless of genetic propensities, are developed within sets of meanings and values that we call "culture." Studies of infant and early childhood learning and behavior attest to the reality of our cultures in forming who we are.

It is a basic tenet of anthropological knowledge that all normal human beings have the capacity to learn any cultural behavior. The American experience with immigrants from hundreds of different language and cultural backgrounds who have acquired some version of American culture traits and behavior is the clearest evidence of this fact. Moreover, people of all physical variations have learned different cultural behaviors and continue to do so as modern transportation moves millions of immigrants around the world.

How people have been accepted and treated within the context of a given society or culture has a direct impact on how they perform in that society. The "racial" worldview was invented to assign some groups to perpetual low status, while others were permitted access to privilege, power, and wealth. The tragedy in the United States has been that the policies and practices stemming from this worldview succeeded all too well in constructing unequal populations among Europeans, Native Americans, and peoples of African descent. Given what we know about the capacity of normal humans to achieve and function within any culture, we conclude that present-day inequalities between so-called "racial" groups are not consequences of their biological inheritance but products of historical and contemporary social, economic, educational, and political circumstances.

American Anthropological Association Statement on "Race" (May 17, 1998). [Note: For further information on human biological variations, see the statement prepared and issued by the American Association of Physical Anthropologists, 1996 (AJPA 101:569-570).]

"PASSING."

This term might best be eliminated from our vocabulary, as it legitimizes the basis for the "one drop rule" of race. To "pass" implies that even though people might look at you and believe that you are "white," you are nonetheless "black"—and should identify yourself as such–if you have an African ancestor lurking in your past. The assumption is not only that race is an objective biological category of distinction, but furthermore that African "blood" somehow overwhelms all other "blood" in determining who a person really is. **(Vikki Bynum, "Exploring the Many Facets of Mixed-Race identity").**

The late Mae Street Kidd, a former "black" representative from Kentucky, exposed the absurdity of the one drop rule and the concept of "passing" when she said,

"I've been passing for black all my life because I'm almost 90 percent white. . . . It's so very obvious that I'm so much whiter than I am black that I have to pretend to be black." **(Wade Hall, Passing for Black: The Life and Careers of Mae Street Kidd (1997), p. 177)**

***

Petition 11082401
Mississippi, Jefferson County
1824
Abstract: Andrew Barland, the son of a white man by a woman of mixed race, was given a good education by his father as well as some property. He states, that, having married into "a respectable white family," he has always been received and treated as a white man. Furthermore, he has served as a juror, given testimony in court, voted, and "enjoyed all the privileges of a free white Citizen." Recently, howerver, a controversy has arisen in a court case when one Joseph Hawk called into question whether Barland, a man of color, should be allowed to testify. Barland writes to the

legislature that "his education, his habits, his principles, and his society are all identified with your views." Barland notes that he owns slaves and therefore "can know no other interest than that which is common to the white population." He asks, therefore, that the state "extend to your petitioner such privileges as his countrymen may think him worthy to possess."

Result: No recorded result.

***

Petition 11683519
Virginia, Prince William County
February 20, 1835
Abstract: In 1834, deputy sheriff Basil Brawner sold William Hyden, who had been jailed as a runaway slave, to one Robert Lipscomb acting as the agent of an unnamed slave trader. When the unnamed trader finally came to town to take a look at Hdyden, he refused to pay. Brawner then asked Colonel James Fewell, a slave trader on his way to Fredericksburg and Richmond, to sell Hyden. Fewell offered Hyden for sale in both locations but to no avail, all interested buyers refusing "to purchase him at any price, on account of his colour all alledging that he was too white." Hyden was returned to Brawner, who later tried to sell him on a court day in Brentsville, but again the several traders present refused "to make any offer for him, alledging that his colour was too light and that he could by reason thereof too easily escape from slavery and pass himself for a free man." As it happened, Hyden did escape, and Brawner now seeks compensation for the "expense that arose from aprehension, confinement, advertising &c." Robert Lipscomb is unable to pay the $452 he bid for Hyden, Brawner argues, and former sheriff Michael Cleary "now stands charged on the books of the Auditor of Public accounts with a large sum of Money which your petitioner will be compelled to pay unless your Honorable body will release him from it, although he has not received nor has he any hope of receiving one cent of the same." Several related documents offer the opinions of

individuals who express their conviction that, from what they had learned of Hyden's background and from what they saw and heard of him, he was a native of New York, born of a white woman, and an educated man.

Result: rejected.

Comments: *Born of a white woman and an educated (black) man...or else* Hyden, *would not have had a racial identity problem. Forced to flee slavery, he tasted freedom and was captured, but that taste of liberty; even on the run was all he needed to plot his course back to freedom passing as he could for a white-person.*

***

Petition 20682112
Georgia, Scriven County
1821

Luke H. Smith sues Alexander Douglass for slander and $2,000 in damages. He claims to have maintained a good reputation in his community and among his peers until August 1820, when Douglass, within the presence of others, alleged that the petitioner is "a damned negro." Because of these accusations, Smith contends, he "is very much prejudiced, hurt, & damnified in his good name, fame, credit & reputation." He sues for damages. **Result:** nonsuit.

***

Petition 20682115
Georgia, Screven County
April, 1822

Abstract: Luke H. Smith sues Doughlass Black for $2,000 in damages. Smith claims to have maintained a solid reputation in the community and enjoyed the esteem of his neighbors until Black, within "the presence and hearing of" others, accused him of being a "damned negro." Smith claims that this accusation has severely damaged his reputation and standing in the community, and in his business affairs. He sues for damages. In his answer, a related document, Black contends that "the words if spoken" by him were "at a time when he was an infant and under the age of twenty one, and not liable to be sued in this Court in his own name."

Result:

***

Comments: *A Jest's prosperity lies in the ear of him that hears it, never in the tongue of him who makes it.* **-William Shakespeare**.

Petition 20882415
Louisiana, Orleans
March 29 – December 20, 1824
Abstract: The petitioner is Maria Townes, a minor, who claims that she is a free white woman held as a slave and daily put up for sale in New Orleans by a man named Reed [Reves]. She prays the court that "she may be adjudged to be free" and that Reed be condemned to pay $1,000 in damages for "unjustly" keeping her in detention, plus costs of suit. She also prays the court to order her sequestration by the sheriff until termination of the suit. As a destitute minor, assisted by a curator ad litem, she is asking to be allowed to sue "in forma pauperis." A related document suggests that Maria's mother was a mulatto woman and a slave in Virginia, where Reed had purchased Maria [Original in English and French].

Result: partially granted.

Comments: *Partially granted. The details are unknown but with documents that suggests that Maria's mother was a mulatto slave (half-white) she would have been at least one-third black; getting that one-third from a black grandfather, making her a so-called quadroon, a person of one-quarter African ancestry, that is one biracial parent ((African and Caucasian) and one Caucasian parent; in other words, one African and three Caucasian grandparents ...which was used, along with the status of her mother, to condemn her to slavery. By partially granted, I hope it meant that she was at least granted her freedom.*

***

Petition 20883931
Louisiana Orleans Parish
July 10, 1839
Abstract: James Thompson represents that, on the 6th of April 1839, his "quatroon" slave, Mary Jane, boarded the ship Orleans and was carried away to New York City. According to Thompson, the captain of the ship, S. Sears, permitted Mary Jane "to eat at table with white people" and in other respects treated her "as an equal of white people." In addition, while in New York City, Sears allowed Mary Jane to associate with abolitionists. Thompson contends that Mary Jane used to be a "good faithful and trusty house servant;" she is now "entirely and totally unfit for such a trust or for any useful purpose." Furthermore, Mary Jane had with her $100 and several articles of clothing belonging to him when she boarded the ship. Thompson therefore seeks $1,000 in damages from S. Sears and the owners of the ship Orleans. In addition, claiming a privilege on the ship to secure his demand, he asks the court to sequester the ship.

Result: partially granted.

***

Petition 20884301
Louisiana Orleans Parish 1843
Abstract: Durham Spalding sues Captain George Taylor and the owners of the Steamer Missouri for the loss of a twenty-three-year-old slave named Felix. Felix was carried out of the state on the Steamer Missouri and "has never, since, been in your petitioner's possession." Spalding argues that "the property, to him was very valuable, and that he has frequently been offered for it the Sum of Fifteen hundred Dollars." Spalding prays for compensation. Related testimonies reveal that Felix was thought to be a white man by all those who met him, and that he was allowed to hire himself out, travel up and down the Mississippi river on steamboats, and to collect his own wages.

Result: granted; appealed; reversed.

***

Petition 20984302
Maryland, Baltimore County
October 25, 1843
Abstract: Elizabeth Tinges married her husband, William Tinges, twelve or thirteen years ago. She claims that "in order to induce her to enter in to the said contract of Marriage She was basely and wickedly imposed upon, and made the victim of a most outrageous fraud." After being married she learned that her husband, "instead of being a white man is a mulatto and in reality had been born a slave." She says that all her acquaintances have shunned her, believing that she knew he was a mulatto all along and did not care. When she approached William Tinges with her discovery, she was met with "brutal invective and evasion." She claims that he treats her cruelly, frequently becomes inebriated, and is "a visitor of houses of ill fame and other places of infamy and disgrace." Elizabeth Tinges asks the court to subpoena William Tinges and to issue a divorce decree. In his answer, William Tinges counters that his wife knew he was a mulatto and that, in fact, she told him before their marriage that he was "White enough for her."

Result: No recorded result.

Comments: As indicated in the petition, there is no record of the results. However, if we are to take the accusations at face value and give plausible cause to each of the complainants. Then, it would seem unreasonable that she would not know William was a Mulatto. She must have known something of his parents, relatives or ancestors.

Conveniently, it seems that the gossip started around the time William started acting up. This is one of those situations where you are tempted to say he began to "show his true colors," BUT FOR THE FACT as many white men as free blacks and mulatto men drank too much and had numerous bouts of infidelity and domestic abuse.

***

Petition 21185902
Missouri, St. Louis County
October18, 1859 – May 7, 1863
Abstract: Louisa Lewis seeks permission to sue as a poor person to establish "the right of herself, and of her minor son George to freedom." Louisa claims that seventeen years ago her mother Lizzie, alias Elizabeth Dickson, a free person of color, purchased Louisa "for the purpose, and on the condition that she should be free." Louisa argues that, inasmuch as it is illegal for free persons of color to own slaves in Missouri, the "purchase of petitioner by her mother operated as a deed of manumission." Fourteen-year-old George was born three years after "the emancipation of your petitioner" and has lived as a free person his entire life. Henry W. Hart, the administrator of Elizabeth Dickson's estate, now holds Louisa and George as slaves. Louisa asks the court to recognize her status as a free woman. Depositions in the court record reveal that George, whose color is "nearly white," attended "common school with white children." Before her mother's death, Louisa spent time in Chicago with her husband, a former slave manumitted by St. Louis mayor, John How. A deposition from Martha Brown intimates that Louisa passed for white while in Chicago.

Result: petition granted; supplemental petition filed; granted; appealed; affirmed.

***

Petition 21485723
Tennessee, Giles County
August 31 – September 16, 1857
Abstract: Margaret J. Mason, administratrix of her late husband's estate, prays for permission to sell a slave. She informs the court that her husband, William T. Mason, died in 1855, leaving an estate that includes slaves, stock in the Richland Manufactory Company, cash, and other assets. Mason asserts that "most of said slaves are very valuable, & productively employed in the Richland Cotton Mills." She is

concerned, however, about a slave named Green, "who is white & could easily pass himself for a white man anywhere." She confides that she "has good reason to believe that said slave is restless & dissatisfied with the condition of slavery, and contemplates an escape." Admitting that should Green try to run away, he would probably succeed, "both from his color and general appearance as from his intelligence & shrewdness." Requesting that the slave be sold, Mason maintains that she would receive a better price for Green if she could take him to Nashville and put him "in the hands of a trader" rather than sell him "at public outcry in this market."

Result: partially granted.

Comments: *When I read petitions like this one, I am amazed by the obsession of the slaver with color. I call this the Goldielocks paradox! Mr. Green was black, but not to black; white, but not to white; restless, intelligent & shrewd, traits that struck fear in the hearts of slavers.*

***

Petition 21685309
Virginia, Petersburg City 1853
Abstract: Edward Hugh Caperton asks permission to sell his two slaves. He informs the court that his mother, Martha J. Caperton, left him property that included a slave named Cary and that his father, George W. Caperton, left him a slave named Queen Ann. Averring "that both of the said negroes have very bad characters," Edward complains that Cary "is almost white and has made attempts to run away & indeed at one time got far from home before he was arrested," thus instilling a fear that Cary will flee to a free state. He also asserts that Queen Ann is a "notorious thief having been before the mayor & whipped at the whipping post and besides your complt has reason to suspect that she has destroyed one or more of her illegitimate children at their birth." Based on these reasons and the fact that "negroes now command very high prices," Caperton surmises "that his interest would be promoted by a sale of said negroes." He

accordingly prays that the court will order his guardian "to sell the said slaves."

Result: granted.

***

Petition 11000016
Mississippi, Jefferson County
Legislative Papers, Petitions, and Memorials
1817-1839
Abstract: A free man of color named Malachi Hagins states that he is descended from several generations of free ancestors. His grandmother was a white woman, and his father died in the American Revolution fighting on behalf of the "Revolted Colonies." Hagins notes that he moved to Mississippi twenty-two years ago, married a white woman, fathered nine children, and acquired land, cattle, and nine slaves. He is now subject to being driven from his country and having his property confiscated and his life put in jeopardy "for want of the guardian protection of the Laws of the Land." He asks for an act to give him "security & protection, such rights and liberties" as the legislature might deem "humane, politick and right."

Result: No recorded result.

***

Petition 11082401
Mississippi Jefferson County
1824
Abstract: Andrew Barland, the son of a white man by a woman of mixed race, was given a good education by his father as well as some property. He states, that, having married into "a respectable white family," he has always been received and treated as a white man. Furthermore, he has served as a juror, given testimony in court, voted, and "enjoyed all the privileges of a free white Citizen." Recently, howerver, a controversy has arisen in a court case when one Joseph Hawk called into question whether Barland, a man of color, should be allowed to testify. Barland writes to the

legislature that "his education, his habits, his principles, and his society are all identified with your views."

Barland notes that he owns slaves and therefore "can know no other interest than that which is common to the white population." He asks, therefore, that the state "extend to your petitioner such privileges as his countrymen may think him worthy to possess."

Result: No recorded result.

***

Petition 11086601
Mississippi Simpson County
October 8, 1866
Abstract: Citizens of Simpson County ask that Lewis Dixon be granted all the rights and privileges of white men. Dixon's mother was white; he was three generations removed from the "African race;" and he had never associated with "recently made Freedmen."

Result: No recorded result.

***

Petition 11279303
North Carolina
December 26, 1793
Abstract: Darby Henagan seeks to emancipate "two molatto slaves almost white" named Penny and Ned whose mother and grandmother served him meritoriously for years. "Advanced in life," Henagan acknowledges his "abhorrence & detestation of seeing persons of mixed blood in slavery which are almost white." He therefore "most ardently prays your Honble body to pass a Law to liberate the aforesaid Molatto children." **Result:** House, Senate: read, referred.

***

Petition 11279511
North Carolina
November 13, 1795
Abstract: Charles Johnson represents that "he has and holds a Certain boy of Colour of about four years of age as a slave, being born as such by the Laws of this Country." He further declares that the child's "white blood so far prevails, that it is almost impossible for any person to discern that he is of mix'd blood." The petitioner, from "principles both of policy and Humanity," therefore prays "that the said boy by the name of Gustavus Adolphus Johnson should be freed & Liberated, and that you will pass a Law for that purpose."

Result: referred to Committee on Emancipation.

***

Petition 11280005
North Carolina Cumberland County
Date December 5, 1800
Abstract: Gurdon Deming represents that "he is the owner of a Certain woman named Lucy and her child Laura." Deming describes the history of Lucy as "a romantic one" in that she "is the daughter of a free white woman" and that "to conceal this circumstance, so as to protect the reputation of the real mother, Lucy at her birth was placed in charge of a woman a slave of one John Selph." He further avers that said Selph intended to manumit Lucy but his death "being sudden and his estate proving insolvent, his intentions were frustrated." As "Lucy in colour is perfectly White, and cannot be distinguished from the purest of the race," Deming prays that a law be passed "authorizing the Emancipation of the said Lucy, and her child Laura." The petitioner also adds that Lucy's "associations have been distinct from the coloured population and her whole demeanor that of the whites to which class she evidently belongs."

Result: No recorded result.

***

Petition 11280006
North Carolina Cumberland County
December 5, 1800
Abstract: Thirty-nine citizens of Cumberland County "cheerfully join in" the petition of Gurdon Deming to emancipate his slave Lucy and her daughter Laura. They avow that many "of your petitioners Who have known Lucy more recently have no hesitation in Saying that from her general appearance they verily believe that She is of pure White blood too White to be a slave and ought to be manumitted." The petitioners believe "that in doing so, you will do an act of Justice to an unfortunate woman illegally held in bondage, who for more than Eighteen Years has faithfully performed the Menial duties of a Servant without murmuring tho often importuned to assert her freedom."

Result: granted.

COMMENTS: *The examination of these petitions makes, on the face of it the quite reasonable assumption that a race of people had been created, that were difficult to exclude from social representation. In almost all cases the free white guardian was attempting to affect the lineal status of their offspring or mulatto relatives.*

***

Petition 11383702
South Carolina Barnwell District/Parish
December 1, 1837
Abstract: William Dunn asks to emancipate a twelve-year-old slave, William, whose mother is "light yellow" and whose father is white. Dunn declares that said child is "so very white and of so good a complexion, as not to create even a suspicion on the mind of the most critical observer" that he is a person of color. He further avers that the said William "has in his raising been kept, thus far, separate and apart, from the Society of coloured people, and has, consequently not imbibed any of the principles or habits peculiar to them." The petitioner insists that "it is inconsistent, with [his] feelings ... to retain in slavery, a person, who approximates, so closely

in identity of colour, habits and appearance to that of the white man." He therefore prays that an act be passed "granting your petitioner leave and authorizing him to emancipate the said little Boy William with permission for him to remain in the State."

Result: referred to Judiciary Committee.

***

Petition 11285202
North Carolina Columbus County
November 15, 1852
Abstract: William Gore and others ask to free Gore's slave Rachel because she "is very white and so little distinguishable from white persons, that it would Shock our feelings, that she Should be compelled to remain in bondage." In addition, three-year-old Rachel is "humble and obedient and of good character."

Result: Rejected.

***

Petition 11383702
South Carolina Barnwell District/Parish
December 1, 1837
Abstract: William Dunn asks to emancipate a twelve-year-old slave, William, whose mother is "light yellow" and whose father is white. Dunn declares that said child is "so very white and of so good a complexion, as not to create even a suspicion on the mind of the most critical observer" that he is a person of color. He further avers that the said William "has in his raising been kept, thus far, separate and apart, from the Society of coloured people, and has, consequently not imbibed any of the principles or habits peculiar to them." The petitioner insists that "it is inconsistent, with [his] feelings ... to retain in slavery, a person, who approximates, so closely in identity of colour, habits and appearance to that of the

white man." He therefore prays that an act be passed "granting your petitioner leave and authorizing him to emancipate the said little Boy William with permission for him to remain in the State."

Result: referred to Judiciary Committee.

***

Interracial relationships were from the outset an arena for personal and institutional conflicts. The contradiction is in its prevalence as a common practice between the races and its critical rejection by the institutions that were of the people...for the people and by the people! Its prevalence increasingly embittered the law makers and dramatized the characteristics of forced segregation in the United States. How can it be that if "majority rule" democracy represents supreme political maturity and judgment, yet to the same degree did not apply to integration? The majority of Americans free and enslaved wanted to integrate and throw off the bonds of slavery but the institution would not allow it...it took a war....the shedding of blood to allow the mixing of blood in America...and some fought on after that terrible war.

***

THY BROTHER'S KEEPER?

According to the first census of 1790, 36 out of 102, or 35.2 percent of the free Black heads of household held slaves in Charleston City, and by 1800, one out of every three free blacks owned slaves. Between 1820 and 1840 the percentage of slaveholding heads of household ranged from 72.1 to 77.7 percent, however, by 1850 the percentage fell to 42.3 percent. Therefore, it is a historical fact that Blacks owned black slaves in numbers disproportionate to their representation in society. This paradox has led some people in recent history to determine that slavery must not have been that bad for blacks, if they chose to enslave their own color and in some cases enslaved their own children. This paradox, like a slight of hand trick takes society's eye off of the ball.

The real culprits behind slavery in America were not the Blacks who owned slaves, nor the fact that the first case of official technical slavery in America was black-own-black, it is the intricate reality that Blacks, free; enslaved and slave owners had no say so in the making of the laws that established; enforced and maintained slavery in America...likewise, the laws that freed them were not written based on their consultation. It was what it was, a failed social; economic and moral institution.

***

Petition 20883031
Louisiana Orleans Parish
October 18- December 27, 1830
Abstract: Isaac T. Preston presents to the court that William Zabrisky, a free man of color, fraudulently "dispossessed" him of his two slaves, twenty-one-year-old Judea and fourteen-year-old Joe. Preston alleges that Zabrisky entered his house and enticed his slaves to leave, intending to take

them into his possession. He claims to have amicably asked Zabrisky to restore the slaves, but Zabrisky has refused to do so. He therefore asks the court to sequester the slaves pending resolution of the suit and, after due delay, to condemn Zabrisky to return the slaves and pay him $2,000 in damages. Related testimonies and the conclusions of the related judgment reveal that Zabrisky and Preston had entered into a tentative agreement to trade slaves on a trial basis. Zabrisky would exchange Judea and Joe for Preston's three slaves, Melissa and her two children. Zabrisky, however, decided not to complete the deal and to end the experiment; upon Preston's resistance to return Judea and Joe, he took matters in his own hands. **Result:** denied; appealed; reversed.

***

Petition 20883815
Louisiana Orleans Parish
May 8-22, 1838
Abstract: William Kincaid and his wife, Nancy Tinsley Kincaid, free people of color, petition to get payment from the sheriff in a case involving a runaway slave. The Kincaids represent that, earlier in the year, a court order directed the sheriff, Frederick Buisson, to seize and sell a slave named Antoine, who had been mortgaged to them by Manuel Fleret and Virgile Perry as security on a debt. The Kincaids contend, however, that Buisson exhibited such gross negligence in the execution of his duties that he "suffered" Antoine to run away. Three months have elapsed and Antoine has not been found; he is presumed to have left the state. The Kincaids therefore pray for an order condemning Buisson to pay them $2,000 to cover the writing-off of the debt plus expenses. Related testimony reveals that Antoine may have drowned in the swamp while attempting to escape.

Result: set aside.

***

Petition 20883818
Louisiana Natchitoches Parish
May 10, 1838-November 5, 1844

Abstract: Jean Baptiste Cécile, a free man of color, seeks to cancel the sale of his two slaves to a free woman of color named Augustine Saint Denis. Cécile represents that Saint Denis, aided and abetted by her slave named Cyprienne [Cyprien], a "statu libri" believed to be her husband, had cheated him out of his two slaves. He charges that, while he was intoxicated on the night of the 4th of April 1838, Saint Denis induced him to sell his two slaves to her, Henry and Mary, by representing to him that he could thus avoid seizure of the slaves by his creditors. According to Cécile, Saint Denis led him to believe that, after the sale, he could retain possession of the slaves and, to seal the deal, a lease was signed by which he agreed to pay Saint Denis a monthly fee for the services of the two slaves and Saint Denis gave him a will whereby she bequeathed the two slaves to him in case of her death. The day after the sale, Cécile became "sensible of his error" and tried to cancel the sale. Saint Denis agreed to do so, but asked that the matter be allowed to stand a few days. However, Saint Denis never cancelled the sale. Instead, she took possession of the slaves for whom she had never paid Cécile the purchase price of $1,100. Cécile therefore seeks an order declaring the sale null and void and decreeing him the owner of the slaves. A number of related documents reveal that Cécile was indeed near insolvency and that he and Saint Denis had concocted a plan to avoid seizure of his property by creditors, but that Saint Denis had then carried the plan one step further by defrauding her own accomplice.

Result: denied; appealed & remanded; denied; new trial granted; found for plaintiff; new trial granted; found partially for plaintiff and against defendant in favor of intervenors; new trial denied; appealed; partially sustained.

***

Petition 20884044
Louisiana Orleans Parish
March 24, 1840-January 24, 1842
Abstract: Pierre St. Luc Ricard, a free man of color of the parish of West Baton Rouge, seeks compensation for the loss of a slave. Ricard claims that his slave James died "in consequence of the carelessness negligence & want of skill of the Captain & other officers having command of the steam Boat John Linton in her trip from New Orleans to Red River." According to Ricard, James was aboard a ferry flat boat when the steam boat ran into it near the Western shore of the Mississippi in the parish of West Baton Rouge. James was thrown from the boat and immediately drowned. Ricard asserts that James was worth the sum of $2,000. He prays that the captain of the boat, Peter Frank Kimball whom he erroneously calls D. T. Kimball, and Edward H. Satterfield, the man he believes to be an owner, be held responsible for the death of his slave. He asks the court to order the defendants to pay him the sum of $2,000 plus $30 per month for the loss of James's services.

Result: granted; appealed.

***

Petition 20884719
Louisiana St. Landry Parish
February 5, 1847-June 4, 1849
Abstract: Jane Davis, a free mulatto woman, seeks to be "separated in bed and board" from her husband, William Edmunds, a free man of color. The couple intermarried in 1835 and "lived together happily and contentedly" for many years. Notwithstanding her "dutiful and affectionate" behavior, Jane now charges that William has broken his "marital vows" by abandoning, deceiving, and maltreating her, and that he is at the moment in "the embraces" of another woman. Moreover, William now denies that he and Jane were ever "united in the bonds of Lawful wedlock," thus

publicly "defaming and blackening" his wife's reputation. He even induces people to believe that Jane is "of doubtful fame & chastity."

Jane asserts that their living together is insupportable; she therefore seeks a separation from her husband and financial support during her "natural life." Related depositions provide detailed information about life among free people of color in Philadelphia, where Jane lived for some time.

Result: motion to dismiss.

***

Petition 20884535
Louisiana Orleans Parish
November 24, 1845-August 7, 1846
Abstract: Due to her husband's insolvency and misappropriation of her property, Polly Stewart, a free woman of color, petitions for a separation of property. Prior to her 1843 marriage to William Stewart, a free man of color, Polly owned a "lot of ground" with a two-story frame house in New Orleans and a slave named Rachiel, altogether worth $3,500. She also owned "certain household furniture" worth $300. Polly informs the court that, since their marriage, William has "not acquired any thing nor assisted in supporting her." Instead, William has "asserted title" to Polly's property and has "forcibly entered into and taken possession of the same." She charges that William has rented her property out as a "depot for the sale & keeping of slaves." In addition, William has allowed the property to deteriorate and has changed the locks, retaining the keys for his own use. Polly petitions the court to have the house and lot sequestered by the sheriff. She also prays for a separation of property from her husband and asks to be granted the "administration and sole control of her paraphernal property."

Result: granted.

***

Petition 20884745
Louisiana Plaquemines Parish
March 2, 1847- November 20, 1848

Abstract: Harriette Duplessis, a woman of color, petitions for her freedom. Harriette represents that, although she was freed under the 1833 last will and testament of her late master, a free man of color named Martin Duplessis, she was sold in 1842 by Martin's heirs to a free man of color named Casimir Duplessis. Claiming to have an "undoubtful right to her freedom," Harriette prays that the court will declare the sale to Casimir Duplessis null and void. She also asks the court to condemn Casimir to free her and her children. Finally, she reserves the right to recover the value of her services for the time she was detained in slavery [Original in English and French; French version incomplete].

Result: granted; appealed; affirmed.

Comments: The history of oppression during the slavery era, is a history of endeavors to cheat re-shape and re-package human nature. Slavery is man's voluntary ascension to the status of master. This petition shows that it made no difference whether the masters were white or black, they, for the most part voluntarily bereaved themselves of fairness and reason and made themselves masters of other men's lives. As masters, they alone had the prerogative to chain a right; whip freedom and tar and feather justice.

***

Petition 11083005
Mississippi, Jefferson
November 23, 1830

Abstract: Working and saving for many years, free man of color Jeremiah Gill purchased his wife, Amy, and daughter, Betsey, from one Caleb Reed. Now being "advanced in years," Jeremiah Gill asks the legislature for an act of emancipation for his family. He feared that if he were to die his wife and daughter might "through the tyranick grasp and relentless cupidity of some unfeeling wretch, be deprived of that portion of liberty, which the sweat of your petitioner's humble brow has purchased for them." In a related petition, filed the same year, one Theodore Richey presented Amy, whom he calls Ama, for emancipation, claiming her as his property. In this petition, Jeremiah Gill's prayer is granted; Amy and Betsey are set free and are given the last name of Gill. At the same time, the legislature also grants freedom to another slave named Rachel, whose emancipation was sought by one Lewis L. Glover.

Result: granted.

***

Petition 11279207
North Carolina Craven County
November 22, 1792
Abstract: John Moore, "a free negro man," seeks to liberate his children, "who are unfortunately illegitimate being born of a negro woman slave belonging to himself." Having worked for fifty years to accumulate a small amount of property, Moore laments that he "is informed that under their present disabilities they would not be intitled by Law to any property which he might have at his Death." He therefore prays that he be granted "Relief by passing an Act to liberate his children."

Result: granted.

***

Petition 11279504
North Carolina Anson County
January 8, 1795
Abstract: Abraham Jones, a free person of color, discloses that he "labours under the unhappy disadvantage of having Seven children by a woman Slave formerly the property of one Westerfield, with whom he has intermarried, and who he has since bought and purchased as his own property." Jones is fearful that his said children "are in danger of being continued in bondage or may be after your petitioner's death without some legal provision made in their favour by the

General Assembly." He therefore prays that his seven children "to wit; Isaac Jones, Jacob Jones, Susanna Jones, John Jones, Abraham Jones, Thomas Jones, and Lewis Jones may be emancipated and from henceforth enjoy the protection and benefits of the laws and constitution of this State, in the same manner as others of their colour who were born free."

Result: rejected.

***

Petition 11279701
North Carolina Anson County
November 24, 1797
Abstract: Abraham Jones, a free "mixt Blooded man," avows that "about forty years past he purchased a Certain Woman of Coller by the name of Lydia of one John Westerfield & paid honestly for her & hath Since had Six Children by said Woman." Jones expresses "very great uneasyness" concerning the possibility that "when your Petitioner dyed his Wife & Children woud be Slave." He therefore prays that "your Honourable Body Will take my Case into your Consideration & give your Petitioner Such Relief as in your Wisdom shall seam meet." Twenty-nine subscribers attest that Jones "hath always behaved himself as a man of Choler ought to do & further supports the carrecter of an honest Industrous man & think his case to be [heard] and ought to be Redrest by passing a law of Liberation."

Result: rejected.

***

Petition 11279805
North Carolina
November 19, 1798
Abstract: John Carruthers Stanly, "a man of mixed blood," recounts that Alexander and Lydia Stewart, "in consideration of the long, faithful & meritorious services of your petitioner,"

sought and received a licence from the Craven County Court "to sett your petitioner free"; the said licence enabled them to execute a deed of manumission "whereby they [did] give, grant, & confirm unto your petitioner his freedom liberty & emancipation." Fearing "that some accident may deprive him of the evidence of his emancipation & thereby of the fruits of his honest industry," Stanly prays that a law be passed to "confirm, establish and Secure to your petitioner his Freedom."

Result: granted.

***

Petition 11279812
North Carolina Pasquotank County
November 21, 1798
Abstract: Lemuel Overnton, "of mix'd Blood but free Born," acknowledges that he "did faithfully Serve in the Last American Warr with Great Britain." He further reveals that, "by Consent," he was able to marry a slave woman named Rose and "had my Eldest Son John by her." Overton states that he was able to purchase said Rose and John and that he has a second son named Burdock. The petitioner prays that his case be taken into consideration and that his wife and two sons be emancipated and called "after his own name Overnton." **Result:** Senate, House: read, referred.

***

Petition 11280004
North Carolina Montgomery County
November 28, 1800
Abstract: Thirty-two citizens of Montgomery County support the petition of Daniel Shad, a free person of color, who seeks to emancipate his family. They report that Shad, "since his emancipation in the year 1798," purchased his wife Betty and that "since that time she has had one child by the name of Winny." They therefore "humbly prayeth your Honourable Body to take this case into your wise consideration and emancipate his wife, and child, by the

name of Betty Shad & her Child by the name of Winny Shad."

Result: favorable.

***

Petition 11280104
North Carolina Chowan County
November 28-30, 1801
Abstract: Madelene St. Risque, a free woman of color of Edenton, represents that "she was sometime past intermarried with a negro man named Major, then the slave of Henry Eelbeck" and that in September last she "purchased all right and title which said Henry had in the said Major." St. Risque now "humbly prays that your Honorable body would condescend to take the premises into consideration and pass such Act as may appear, to your Honorable body most fit to emancipate the said Major, your humble Petitioners husband." **Result:** granted.

***

Petition 11283305
North Carolina Martin County County
November 23, 1833
Abstract: Ned Hyman, the former slave of the late Samuel Hyman, represents that "by his faithfulness and extraordinary attention to his masters business and interest secured his esteem and favor and obtained his sincere wishes that your petitioner should be freed." Hyman recounts, however, that "the nearest your petitioner has been able to approach an end so disirable to his decd master is, to have had the title to your petitioner vested in your petitioners wife," Elizabeth Hagans, a free woman of color. The petitioner avers that he "has had the good fortune to accumulate an estate worth from five to six thousand dollars; consisting of Lands chiefly Live stock negroes and money the right & title to all which except the money is

vested" in his wife Elizabeth. The father of three children, Hyman "together with his wife Elizabeth" therefore pray that an act be passed "for his benefit and relief." **Result:** are unknown.

***

Petition 11283808
North Carolina Wake County
November 26, 1838
Abstract: Henry Patterson, a free person of color, seeks to free his wife whom he has purchased. Patterson, "a bricklayer & Plasterer by trade," asserts that "he & his said wife have been brought up in the City of Raleigh and as to character for industry, quietness & good order in general he appeals for himself & his wife to all the respectable inhabitants of this City." Fearing "that if he were to die without a Will his Brothers & Sisters would become the owners of his wife & she might be sold a slave for life for their debts," he also submits that "if he were to make a will he cannot liberate her, nor make any other disposition of her according to law." Patterson therefore states that "to your Hon Body alone can he look for help & redress."

Result: House: referred to committee

***

Petition 11284602
North Carolina Wake County
November 28, 1846
Abstract: John Malone, a fifty-six-year-old free black man living in Raleigh, "is anxious to emancipate and set free from Slavery his said wife & son Edmund before he dies." Malone represents that, "by hard work and close economy," he "has been able to lay by a little money and property and though a free negro he has done this without exciting the suspicion of white gentlemen against his honesty, but so that he may

appeal to the whole community in favour of his claims to a good reputation." He further states that he applied "a part of his earnings ... to the purchase of his wife Cherry and more recently to the purchase of their son Edmond." The petitioner therefore "earnestly beseeches the General Assembly of North Carolina to set free his wife Cherry and Son Edmund by the respective names of Cherry Malone and Edmond Malone" and that they be allowed to remain in the state.

Result: committee favorable; laid on table.

***

Petition 11285201
North Carolina Wayne County
December 17, 1852
Abstract: Five residents of Wayne County join Hilary Croom, "who was born of a woman of respectable parentage though his father was reputed to have been a slave of Colour," in requesting that Croom's three children "be free at their arriving to the age of twenty one years" and that they all be allowed to remain in the state. The white petitioners boast that Croom, alias Coor, "is one of the best blacksmiths we have" and that he "sustains a fair industrious character." They further report that he was previously expelled from the state of Alabama and that now he faces yet another law requiring him to emigrate from his home state or pay a heavy fine. The petitioners therefore pray that "Hilary Croom be suffered to remain with us." **Result:** referred to committee.

***

Petition 11285401
North Carolina Richmond County
November 2, 1854
Abstract: Twenty-six Richmond County residents ask that the son of James Dunn, "an honest & industrious man," be emancipated. They state that Dunn "was formerly a slave but by his energy he bought himself and then his Mother & wife and afterward his son

Louis." Noting that Dunn is now "old & desires to leave his Son Free," the petitioners pray that it may "be the pleasure of the Legislature to Set him Free."

Result: No recorded result.

***

Petition 11382109
South Carolina Laurens District/Parish
1821
Abstract: Allen Kelley, a free person of color and a blacksmith by trade, states that "he purchased in the year 1821 his son George a Slave for whom he paid the Sum of Six hundred and four dollars." Kelley prays that he be granted "permission to indulge in so humane and desireable an object in manumitting & setting free his said son George Kelley."

Result: No recorded result.

***

Petition 11382705
South Carolina Charleston District/Parish
November 6, 1827
Abstract: William Lance represents that fifty-five-year-old Abigail Jones, a free woman of color, moved from Charleston to New York City in 1823 "with her daughter Ann Deas and two grandchildren Abigail Jones Lee and John Lee, also free persons of color and natives of Charleston ... taking with them a girl named Martha, a Slave, as a Servant." He further reports that Abigail's husband Jehu "has always continued to reside in Charleston." The petitioner states that "the said Jehu Jones is far advanced in years, being of the age of Fifty Eight Years, and is anxiously desirous of passing the remainder of his days in his native land, where he has always lived ... and is equally solicitous, as is she herself, that the said Wife with her said family

should be allowed to return to this state." He attests that "the said Jehu and Abigail Jones ... are honest industrious and decent people, and have always sustained that reputation." Lance therefore prays "your honorable body ... to permit her, & her above named family and Servant, to return to her husband, her friends and the country of her birth."

Result: No recorded result.

***

Petition 11382801
South Carolina Richland District/Parish
November 27, 1828
Abstract: James Patterson, a free man of color born in Columbia, seeks to free his wife Sally, his son George, and his daughter Candice. Patterson, "a carpenter by trade," could "not raise a Sufficient Sum to affect that desirable and anxious object" of purchasing his family "until after the passage of the act prohibiting the freeing of slaves." The petitioner reports that he "made the purchase of his wife and Son in 1821 and paid for them One Thousand Dollars a Sum far beyond their value, his Son being at that time about Seven years old, and his wife not worth more than an ordinary female house Servant"; his daughter Candice was born after he had purchased his wife. "Anxious that they should be placed on a footing with himself," Patterson prays that "your Honorable Body ... will take the peculiar circumstances of his case into consideration and make his wife and children free." **Result:** rejected.

***

Petition 11383013
South Carolina York District/Parish
1830
Abstract: Jeremiah Dickey, a free man of color who purchased his freedom, states that during his time as a slave, he had married a mulatto woman, the slave of Robert Manning. Before their marriage, his wife "was delivered of a female child--whose father was a white man." Dickey states

that he purchased Jincey from her owner and now seeks to emancipate her. He therefore prays that he be permitted to free his sixteen-year-old step-daughter "under the name Jensey Dickey."

Result: referred to Judiciary Committee.

***

Petition 11383603
South Carolina Charleston
District/Parish
1836
Abstract: Moses Irvin, a seventy-five-year-old free person of color emancipated for his "faithful services" during the Revolutionary War, seeks to free his wife Harriet and the "two children, which she has born him." Representing that both he and Harriet, whom he purchased, "are far advanced in years," the petitioner "is rendered very unhappy by the situation of his children, who are the persons that he would leave what little he has to, but who are in danger of being seized after his death as vacant property - and confiscated for the use of the State." He therefore "humbly asks your attention to his appeal to your humanity" and "prays that you would be pleased to sanction his children's freedom by allowing them to follow the condition of their father."

Result: No recorded result.

***

Petition 11383805
Richland District/Parish
1838
Abstract: "By a Long life of Care and industry," James Paterson, a free person of color, purchased his wife, Sarah, and his two children, George and Mary. Paterson seeks exemption from the law prohibiting the manumission of slaves and requests permission to free his family, "so that the honest industry, the unwearied pains and untiring efforts of a Father & Husband may not be lossed to him entirely."
Result: rejected.

***

Petition 11384504
South Carolina Abbeville District/Parish
November 15, 1845

Abstract: Priscilla Jessup, a free woman of color, "has considerable property -- That she owns among other things, her husband John, a negro man," whom she purchased in 1834; since his purchase, John's condition, "in consequence of the love and affection which she bears to him has been that only of nominal servitude." Averring John to have always been "industrious, honest faithfull and obedient," the petitioner asks that he be emancipated. Jessup fears "in the event of her death, John ... will fall into other hands in the condition of a slave."

Result:

***

Petition 11385007
South Carolina Spartanburg District/Parish
1850

Abstract: Fifty-four-year-old free mulatto William Jackson, who had lived in the area his entire life, asks to free his wife Lucinda, "a slave though three degrees removed from the African race," and his six children: Susan, Martha, Mary, Berryman, Margaret, and Hosea.

***

Petition 11385702
South Carolina Charleston District/Parish
November 19, 1857

Abstract: William F. Ervin, son of the late Robert Ervin, represents that his father manumitted a slave named Sye "in consideration of his fidelity and good conduct." He further reports that the said Sye, who assumed the name Sye Ervin after his manumission, "accumulated a small property; and with a part of it purchased a female slave with whom he had previously lived as a wife and a female grandchild named

Clarissa." Ervin states that Sye died intestate in 1836 or 1837, leaving a small farm in St. John's Parish, where his said wife lived until her death. He notes that when Sye's granddaughter Clarissa died in 1851, she left six slave children, the eldest age eleven, the youngest an infant. The petitioner declares that he was called upon by his neighbors to attend to the family, who "were left wholly destitute and were in danger of starvation." Averring that he "has taken charge of and supported the said slaves ever since, and has been subjected to considerable expense," the petitioner prays "that all right and Title of the State to the said Property, real and personal, may be released to your petitioner."

Result: No recorded result.

***

Petition 11385705
South Carolina Clarendon District/Parish
1857
Abstract: The heirs of the late Dr. Robert W. Ervin represent that he manumitted a slave named Sye in 1817 and that the said Sye later purchased his wife and his granddaughter named Clarissa. They further state that Clarissa died in 1851, leaving six children: Becky, Jane, Betsy, Leny, Sarah, and Isaac. They also report that Sye has died, seized and possessed of his granddaughter, six great grandchildren, a tract of land, and some cattle and hogs; the estate, however, had no legal heirs and escheated to the state. The heirs charge that William Ervin, another son of the said Robert, took possession of Sye's estate in 1850 or 1851, including the slaves, who until this time were "passing as free." The petitioners, "some being in very moderate circumstances, and others in embarrassing circumstances," reveal that they have frequently asked the said William to secure "the benefit of said slaves or their value" to Louisa Ervin, mother of William Ervin, and widow of Robert Ervin. Asserting that they are equally entitled to the slaves, they ask the legislature to vest the title of the slaves to Robert Ervin's heirs at law and

that the sheriff sell the slaves to the highest bidder and divide the proceeds equally among said heirs.

Result:

***

Deed Book D-2: 385-386
South Carolina; Newberry County.
August 14, 1797

Know all men by these Presents that we John Worthington, Elizabeth Worthington, Elijah Worthington, and Molly Worthington, Joseph Jones and Nancy Jones, John Abernathy and Rhonda Abernathy, Thomas W. Waters and Fanny Waters and Chesley Davis, Samuel Davis, Thomas Davis and Jesse Davis and Molly Davis, all of us joint heirs and legatees of Mary Davis, deceased do for divers good cause and consideration that proper to enfranchise a certain Negro wench named Pat about 40 years old yellow complexion which said Negro wench is our just and right property and we do jointly by these presents free her and her heirs together with her body forever and by these presents to acquit her of all manner of Servitude to us, our heirs, or assigns and she is as far as lays in our power to grant as free as if she had been born free and should this instrument of writing want from not to be set aside but the true intent and meaning of the same to be taken and liberally construed in the favor of the said Negro wench hereunto set our hands and seals 14 August 1797. Signed. Thomas W. Waters, Fanny Waters, John Worthington, Elizabeth (her mark) Worthington, Milly Worthington, Chesley Davis, Samuel Davis, Thomas Davis, Molly Davis, Jesse Davis, Nancy Jones, Joseph Jones, Rhoda Abernathy, John Abernathy. Wit. Thomas Berry, Jacob Berry.

Proved by Jacob Berry 21 April 1798 before D Clary, J. P.

***

Deed Book D-2: 385-386
South Carolina, Newberry County.

431: 2 Aug 1844

GEORGE ROBERTS a free man of color to THOMAS M. ROBERTS; whereas the said GEORGE is owner of two persons of color by name of RICHARD and ZILPHY, children of GEORGE by descent from ELIZABETH ROBERTS, mother of said THOMAS M. ROBERTS; Deed of Gift of RICHARD and ZILPHY.

***

Petition 11385912
South Carolina Charleston District/Parish
July 1, 1859
Abstract: The mulatto children of the late Philip Stanislas Noisette, a white botanist who died in 1835, ask to remain in South Carolina as free persons of color. They state that their father freed them in his will and that "the provisions of this will are perfectly legal, and that there is no question about their freedom, but that they might be required to emigrate." Citing that they were born in the state, the petitioners assert that they "are very unwilling to remove." They further point out that "those who have the public interest most at heart would recognize the propriety of an exception in their behalf that would permit them to remain where they are." The petitioners therefore pray that "they and their issue may be permitted to remain in the State in the condition of free persons of color."

Result: Unknown.

***

Petition 11483319
Tennessee Hardeman County
1833

Abstract: Joshua Thurman represents that "in the year of 1831 he purchased his sister Harriett a Slave from Washington Edgings who then owned her" and that "when he made the purchase it was with the express promise and understanding that he your petitioner would give the said Harriett her freedom, That M Edings refused to sell her upon any other condition." Thurman relates, however, "that before it was in his power to do so, the Honorable General assembly of this State passed a law prohibiting the emancipation of Slaves." He further avows that "the said Harriett is a discreet and industrious girl and has greatly assisted your petitioner in paying for her; for which reason as well as the ties of brotherly love," he is still "desirous to discharge this moral obligation of seting her free." The petitioner therefore "with great deference would Humbly pray your Honorable Body to pass a law to authorise your petitioner to emancipate the said Harriett."
Result: reasonable.

***

Petition 11483320
Tennessee Davidson County
1833
Abstract: Free man of color Stephen Lytle requests permission for himself and for his family to remain in Tennessee. Lytle purchased himself for four hundred dollars from his owner, William Lytle of Nashville; he then purchased his wife, Charity. The couple had a daughter, Mary Shepherd Lytle, and acquired two city lots. On 17 April 1832, Stephen Lytle discovered that he was not by law a free man and that his wife and child were slaves of his master. "He is informed that the second section of the act of 1831, Session acts, page 121.2 prohibits his emancipation & that of his wife & child, 'except on the express Condition,' that he & they shall immediately remove from the state of Tennessee, and unless his master & the master of his wife & child, shall before their 'emancipation enter into bond with good and sufficient security, in a sum equal to their

respective values, Conditioned that they' ...shall forthwith remove from the State of Tennessee." Having enough money to post bond for himself but not enough for his wife and four-year-old daughter, Lytle states that he faces the dilemma of leaving them behind or remaining in Tennessee and facing possible re-enslavement. He asks for relief.

Result: No recorded result.

***

Petition 20184722
Alabama Mobile County
December 9, 1847
Abstract: Margaret Collins, a free woman of color in her eighties, claims that her son, Joseph Collins, had an illegitimate child with his slave, Milly. Joseph gave the boy, named Edward, to Margaret, who in turn entrusted him to her daughter Louisa, wife of Benjamin Laurendine, and referred to as Madam Benjamin. Margaret and other family members treated Edward as a relative, but Louisa hired him out as a slave. After twenty years, Margaret Collins, complaining that she never intended the boy to be a slave, asks that Edward be returned to her and that an accounting of the money made from his hiring out be provided. Louisa Collins Laurendine, who has a sister named Isabel, is referred to as Isabella in parts of the documents.
Result: are unknown.

***

Petition 20882844
Louisiana Orleans Parish
May 19, 1828
Abstract: Josephine Jardelas, a free woman of color and a minor "above the age of puberty," petitions with the assistance of Louis Seré, her "curator ad lites." She presents to the court that the administration of the late Joseph Jardelas's estate is planning to sell three slaves that belong

to her. The three slaves are Elina, also known as Nina, and Elina's two children, four-year-old Maria and eighteen-month-old Charles. Josephine asks the court to order that the register of wills be "enjoined, restrained & prohibited from selling" the slaves and to cite the persons claiming title. She further asks to be recognized "as the sole and lawful mistress" of the three slaves and want them to be sequestered by the sheriff until the case has been decided. Related documents reveal that Josephine was the daughter of the late Joseph Jardelas and Carmelite Boisseau, a free woman of color, and that Joseph Jardelas had lived for many years with Carmelite in the house owned by Carmelite's mother, Manon Boisseau.

Result: granted; appealed; reversed.

***

Petition 20882274
Louisiana Orleans Parish
December 20, 1822-May 10, 1824
Abstract: The petitioner is Rebecca Lunsford, a twenty-eight-year old woman claiming that, although a free person, she is being held in slavery "injustly and illegally" by L. Coquillon. She presents to the court that she "acquired her liberty" by virtue of residing in the free state of Ohio, "at Cincinnati," in the household of one James Riddle. She asks the court to issue a "writ of sequestration" to put her in the custody of the sheriff for hiring out until termination of the suit. She also asks the court to cite L. Coquillon to answer her petition and condemn him to pay her $15 per month for the time she has been with him, plus costs of suit. Above all she asks the court that it "may be ordered adjudged & decreed" that she is a free person and "entitled to her liberty" [Original in English and French].
Result: granted; appealed; upheld.

***

Petition 20882844
Louisiana Orleans Parish
1828-May-19 circa 1829-May-18
Abstract: Josephine Jardelas, a free woman of color and a minor "above the age of puberty," petitions with the assistance of Louis Seré, her "curator ad lites." She presents to the court that the administration of the late Joseph Jardelas's estate is planning to sell three slaves that belong to her. The three slaves are Elina, also known as Nina, and Elina's two children, four-year-old Maria and eighteen-month-old Charles. Josephine asks the court to order that the register of wills be "enjoined, restrained & prohibited from selling" the slaves and to cite the persons claiming title. She further asks to be recognized "as the sole and lawful mistress" of the three slaves and want them to be sequestered by the sheriff until the case has been decided. Related documents reveal that Josephine was the daughter of the late Joseph Jardelas and Carmelite Boisseau, a free woman of color, and that Joseph Jardelas had lived for many years with Carmelite in the house owned by Carmelite's mother, Manon Boisseau.
Result: granted; appealed; reversed.

***

Petition 20882937
Louisiana Natchitoches Parish
1829-October-29 circa 1831-May
Abstract: Louis Derbanne states that his land is being illegally claimed by Francois Metoyer, a free man of color. Derbanne asserts that, in 1801, he purchased a five arpent tract of land at the head of the Cane River from Marguerite, "a free negress." Marguerite had held the land since 1788, when Spanish Colonial Governor Esteban Rodriguez Miro y Sabater "conceded" it to her. Derbanne now asserts that Metoyer "sets up a claim and gives out in speeches that he is the true & legal owner of a portion of the said five arpents front, thereby slandering the title of your petitioner." Derbanne prays that Metoyer pay him $500 in damages and

that he be permanently enjoined "from laying claim to any portion of said five arpents front, or in any manner disturbing the plaintiff in his rights thereto." **Result:** found for defendant.

***

Petition 20883031
Louisiana Orleans Parish
1830-October-18 circa 1830-December-27
Abstract: Isaac T. Preston presents to the court that William Zabrisky, a free man of color, fraudulently "dispossessed" him of his two slaves, twenty-one-year-old Judea and fourteen-year-old Joe. Preston alleges that Zabrisky entered his house and enticed his slaves to leave, intending to take them into his possession. He claims to have amicably asked Zabrisky to restore the slaves, but Zabrisky has refused to do so. He therefore asks the court to sequester the slaves pending resolution of the suit and, after due delay, to condemn Zabrisky to return the slaves and pay him $2,000 in damages. Related testimonies and the conclusions of the related judgment reveal that Zabrisky and Preston had entered into a tentative agreement to trade slaves on a trial basis. Zabrisky would exchange Judea and Joe for Preston's three slaves, Melissa and her two children. Zabrisky, however, decided not to complete the deal and to end the experiment; upon Preston's resistance to return Judea and Joe, he took matters in his own hands.
Result: denied; appealed; reversed.

***

Petition 20883110
Louisiana, Iberville, Parish
1831-June, 27- 1832, November-1

Abstract: Marguerite, a free woman of color, claims that William Janes is indebted to her in the sum of $105. She represents that she hired out her male slave named Urbin to

Janes for the price of $80 per year, plus another $20 for Sunday work. She now alleges that, although Urbin did indeed work on Sundays, Janes has so far refused to pay the agreed upon price and, in addition, owes her $5 from Urbin's hires of the previous year. She therefore prays that Janes be ordered to pay the sum of $105, with interest and "cost according to law."

Result: granted; appealed; partially reversed.

***

Petition 20883121
Louisiana, Orleans, Parish
August 23-25, 1831

Abstract: The widow of Bernard Couvent, a free woman of color, presents to the court and the police jury that she is the owner of two female slaves, forty-year-old Seraphine and forty-five-year-old Fillette, whom she wishes to emancipate in consideration of their faithful services of "a great number of years past," including during "various times" of sickness. She declares that Seraphine and Fillette are "free from any of the defects and blemishes contemplated by Law" in cases of intended emancipation. She therefore asks the court and the police jury to authorize her to emancipate her slaves without having to "furnish the obligation" required by the "Second Section of the act of the [state] Legislature" dated the 25th of March 1831 and without the slaves being compelled to leave the state.

Result: granted.

***

Petition 20883124
Louisiana, Orleans Parish
November - December 19, 1831

Abstract: Pierre Valentin Porée, a free man of color, presents to the police jury that, in 1823, he married a mulatto woman ["griffonnne"]named Ursule, whom he believed had been freed by the last will and testament of her grandmother, a free woman of color named Rosette Brazier. Valentin Porée further presents that Rosette Brazier, having been advised that her last will and testament only conveyed an "eventual hope" but not the reality of freedom, recently made, in his favor, "a donation inter vivos" of Ursule and their four children. The gift was made under the express condition that he would emancipate his family "as soon as it could be done legally." Valentin Porée vouches that Ursule is "a good mother, an affectionate wife," and that she "has constantly behaved according to sound morals and good principles." He therefore asks the police jury to consent to the emancipation of his wife and children, and of "any children that may issue" from their marriage previous to the emancipation.

Result: granted.

***

Petition 20883128
Louisiana, Orleans Parish
July – August 16, 1831

Abstract: Constance des Capucins, a free woman of color and a woman of some means and property, presents to the police jury that she has recently purchased her two-year-old niece named Juliette, from a free woman of color named Bellefine Bardoule, under the condition "sine qua non" that she would immediately proceed to the formalities required by law for emancipation. She explains that she is "possessed of some property" and intends not only to emancipate Juliette but to use her respectable means to educate her. She asks the police jury to authorize her to proceed with the manumission of her niece.

Result: granted.

***

Petition 20883131
Louisiana Orleans Parish
August 26, 1831

Abstract: William Johnson, a long time resident of the city, is a free man of color who has always been employed by the "Gnl Government" or the city. He presents to the court and the police jury that he is the owner of a female slave named Hannah, whom he wishes to emancipate. He declares that Hannah has "rendered him important services at various times in nursing and attending him in sickness," and she has always been "a faithful, honest, sober, and obedient servant." He asks the police jury to authorize him to emancipate Hannah, without compelling him to furnish the obligation required by the 25 March 1831 act of the state legislature and without compelling her to leave the state.
Result: granted.

***

Petition 20883205
Louisiana Pointe Coupee, Parish
May10-26, 1832

Abstract: Claire Décuir, a free woman of color, represents that, upon marrying Louis Severin in 1820, she entered into a marriage contract that stipulated that all her property, "present & future," should be considered "dotal." She claims that, at the time of the marriage, she was possessed of fifteen slaves, a plantation, cattle, and personal property, altogether valued at $4,868. She has, since that time, inherited another $38,200 from Joseph Décuir. Claire Décuir Severin now contends that her husband has sold her plantation, and the state of his affairs is such that her entire dowry is in jeopardy. She therefore prays for a judgment against her husband to recover the full value of her dowry, which amounts to $43,068, and for a separation of property from her husband.

Result: granted.

***

Petition 20883226
Louisiana, Orleans, Parish
August 23, 1832- July 24, 1834

Abstract: Nicolas Desonges, a free man of color, presents to the parish judge and the police jury that he has purchased a forty-six-year-old female slave named Mariguitte for the specific purpose of "obtaining for her the inestimable blessing of freedom." He explains that Mariguitte, whom he calls his "near relative," was born in the family of the late Françoise Hugon, where she continued residing until he recently purchased her. He declares that Mariguitte always served the Hugon family as "an honest faithful slave should do;" and that, moreover, she is "free from any of the misdemeanors and blemishes contemplated by law" in cases of emancipation. He asks the police jury to authorize him to emancipate Mariguitte without asking him "to furnish the obligation required by the last section" of the act of the 16th of March 1830 and without compelling Mariguitte to leave the state.

Result: granted.

***

Petition 20883231
Louisiana, Orleans Parish
May22- December 13, 1832

Abstract: James Dunn, a free man of color, presents to the court and the police jury that he is the "true & legal owner" of his wife, a thirty-five-year-old mulatto woman named Maria, and his two children, ten-year-old Oscar and eight-year-old Jane. He further presents that "from motives of affection" and "in consideration of" Maria's "faithful & important services," he is "anxious that they should be permitted to enjoy the blessings of freedom." James Dunn invokes the provisions of an 1831 legislative act governing the movement of people of color into the state and the mode of emancipating slaves to plead for a residency and age waiver that will allow him to emancipate his family. He also asks to be exempt from furnishing a bond.

Result: granted.

Repository: New Orleans Public Library, New Orleans, Louisiana.

***

**Wills &C. 1784-87, 390-1
Accomack County
September 25, 1787**

Abstract: To all Christian People to whom these presents shall come, Greeting Know Ye that I George Corbin. . . for divers good Causes and Considerations me hereunto moving but more Especially from Motives of Humanity, Justice, and Policy, and as it is Repugnant to Christianity and even common Honesty to live in Ease and affluence by the Labour of those whom fraud and Violence have Reduced to Slavery; (altho' sanctifyed by General consent, and supported by the law of the Land) Have, and by these presents do manumit and set free the following Persons. James, Betty Senior, Jenny Senior, Joshua, son, Betty Junior Bob, Jarry, Spencer, Levin, Abel, Peter, Parker, Lithco, Alicia, Hannah, Amey, Esther, Jenny Junior, Sue, Bob, Liddia, and Will; and that the Identity of the aforesaid persons may in future be better known, and thereby their Right to freedom firmly secured, I do hereby affix to Each and every one of them the Sirname of Godfree. Have and I do hereby for myself my heirs, Executors, and Administrators relinquish all my right or Title of in and unto the Persons aforesaid and their increase forever . . . ; Reserving only to myself . . . the power of holding the Young ones who are under lawful age in such manner only as negroes born free. Proved 31 July 1787.

***

Deed Book 4, LVA Reel #2;
Charles City County, VA
1789-1802

p. 33: Samuel Hargrave of Chas City from mature deliberation and conviction of my own mind being fully persuaded that freedom is the natural right of all mankind and being desirous of doing to others as I would be done by and having 5 Negroes frees Jane aged abt 34, Nancy aged abt 22, William aged abt 13, Sary aged abt 13, Aggy aged abt 8–males at 21 and females at 18 for minors–**recorded 20 Jan 1791**.

***

p. 141: from a sense of its being my duty I [Benjamin Dancy] do hereby emancipate and set free the following Negroes reserving the service of those of them that are under age, the males until 21 and the females till 18–Harry aged 60; Nanny aged 60; Robert aged 48; Betty aged 55; Pat aged 35; Silvy aged 14; Clarissa aged 12; Hannah aged 9; Lucy aged 8; America aged 7; Lucretia aged 3 months– **recorded 19 Sept 1793**.

***

p. 150: Know all men by these presents that I Charles Binns of Chas City and Westover Parish being moved by the principles of humanity and the dictates of my own conscience and do think that all mankind in justice ought to enjoy that inestimable blessing freedom ..by these presents give and grant unto Will a Negro man my slave aged abt 35 yrs his perfect liberty and freedom as if he had been born free–**recorded 19 Dec 1793**.

SLIGHT OF HAND

There is nothing so convincing as a legal opinion, because, it is assumed that the best and brightest minds have rendered the decision and the odd thing about opinions is, "he who states his case first seems right until others view the evidence." (PROVERBS). So, let me give my opinion before you read the following petitions and the cockeyed weight the various legislatures brought to bear on the civil status of black colonist. Their proposals not only suggested something negative about free-black people, but made, too, as aspersion on character.

From the beginning, colonial and later state law makers moved from the haughty aesthetic of the superciliary, to making the astonishing Law of the Unframed Indictment, work to their advantage as white-citizens and Christians. This is the critical equivalent of holding a prisoner without bringing charges. Their opinions condemned generations of black people simply by mentioning it.

Some private white citizens lived among blacks in my opinion, evenly and uninflected and they seemed to have taken higher ground. Then, the law makers introduced a reason, however spurious, that set in motion an avalanche of racist legal actions. The following petitions attest to the successful attempts to insure that people of color had no opportunity to overcome slavery and attain self-sufficiency.

In those troubled days, they toiled laboriously and experienced every form of economic oppression. As an underclass of enslaved and free workers their opportunities became few and their troubles increased as they attempted to participate in the free-market. They had only hoped for success from day to day...Hoped to become the head and became the tail: They worked laboriously and got no satisfaction from their work.

The freedom the colonies wrangled from the tyranny of the Crown failed to create conditions for a larger degree of freedom for its entire people.

Abraham Lincoln said it best:

> "Our progress in degeneracy appears to me to be pretty rapid. As a nation, we began by declaring that "all men are created equal." We now practically read it "all men are created equal, except negroes" When the Know-Nothings get control, it will read "all men are created equal, except negroes, and foreigners, and Catholics." When it comes to this I should prefer emigrating to some country where they make no pretence of loving liberty -- to Russia, for instance, where despotism can be taken pure, and without the base alloy of hypocracy."
> - **August 24, 1855 Letter to Joshua Speed, Abraham Lincoln**.

The dis-enfranchised non-whites were burdened with an acute paramount need to prove themselves and win the favor or the ordainment   of their fellow white citizens who enjoyed the full benefit of the constitution and its values: justice, happiness, and love, the realization of capacities to create new things and experiences and ideas.

***

Petition 10378501
Delaware
December 27, 1785
Abstract: Two hundred and three Quaker petitioners espouse the evil of slaveholding and entreat the legislature "to take the afflicted Case of the oppressed Negroes in this State under your mature Consideration and grant them such Relief as Justice, Humanity, the common natural Rights of

Mankind, and above all the precepts, and Injunctions of the Christian Religion require desiring your Minds may be influenced by divine Wisdom for your Direction."

Result: No recorded result.

***

Petition 10379101
Delaware
January 18, 1791
Abstract: Warner Mifflin, feeling "both sorry and ashamed for" his country, asks the legislature to end slavery on Christian and moral grounds. He upholds "the Necessity of your recommending to the convention the inserting a clause in the constitution, declaring that no more slaves shall be born in this State." Mifflin firmly believes that "without some such clause, it is my judgment, that the Constitution will be disgraced as long as it remains, without this it will be repugnant to the pretended spirit of the Revolution, to say nothing about Christianity." Mifflin also asks the body "to devise some more effectual means to prevent the Salutary Laws already made, from being trampled upon and evaded;" in particular he notes that, in some parts of the state, "free Born, and others entitled to their Liberty by Law, have been thus carry'd away."

Result: No recorded result.

***

Petition 11282710
North Carolina Guilford County
February 2, 1827
Abstract: The petition "of the Female Benevolent Associations of JamesTown, Springfield, and Kennet" calls the legislature's attention to the evil of slavery "which was brought upon us by our forefathers, and is growing with a rapidity which must put at hazard everything that is near and dear to us." The women particularly object to the practices which "degrade the Female Slaves, and render them unacquainted with the honours due to Chastity, both in

speech and behaviour." The petitioners pose that "is it not degrading to humanity to see the back of the matron exposed to public view, (although a Slave) and severely lacerated by the whip for trivial offences?"; they find it "still more shocking to see the mother and her infant offspring separated by a Sale." The petitioners therefore "earnestly entreat" the legislature "to meliorate the condition of this unhappy people as much as possible; by prohibiting the separation of the mothers from their tender infants; and restricting Masters in the administration of corporal punishments from the shameful practice of stripping the black matron's back -- it is a sight too shocking to behold in any Country, and much more in this civilized land of boasted Liberty."

Result: House: read, laid on table.

COMMENTS: *Some historical assumptions by the brave clear thinkers of the Abolitionist Movement began the political reform that wrestled the acceptable idea of enslavement from the minds of most Americans.*

***

Petition 20183702
Alabama, Tallapoosa County
April 6, 1837
Abstract: The children and widow of William Bryant, deceased, seek to be recognized as heirs. They state that in 1818, Bryant left his wife, Rodicy, in Jasper County, Georgia, and moved to Alabama, where he lived the remainder of his life. Bryant owned considerable property when he died, including more than twenty slaves valued at twenty thousand dollars. After Bryant's death, his son, Needham Bryant, moved to Alabama to administer the estate, hiring John H. Peters, to obtain the letters of administration. Peters, however, put the letters in his own name and proceeded to manage the estate. When Peters advertised fifteen slaves and other property for sale, the heirs protested. Peters argued that he had recently found a will which directed him to sell the property and to give one hundred dollars to a

"negro woman Sally & the same amount to several other negroes." In addition, this will stipulated that Bryant's land in Georgia be divided among his children, excluding Needham Bryant, William Bryant Jr. and Bryant's widow from any inheritance. The heirs challenge the validity of the will and ask the court to recognize their claim to Bryant's estate. They also challenge Peters's right to administer the estate. In response, Peters asserts that the complainants "Needham William Nancy Elizabeth Lurany and General J. Bryant are not free white persons capable of being citizens of this state that they are persons of color, commingled with the negro race and wholly incapable of inheriting the property and estate of said William dec. who was a free white man," and that they are not "the next of kin of William." However, it is not on this ground that Peter challenges the right of the Bryant family to inheritance in the remainder of his lengthy answer to the charges.

Result: No recorded result.

***

Petition 11283203
North Carolina Orange County
December 20, 1832
Abstract: Thirty-two citizens of Orange County complain about slaves being present during muster calls and at elections. They purport that "the unavoidable tendency of Musters and Elections to produce [a] distraction in the mind of slave, is a matter of general observation" and "they make him obstinate and sulky, sometimes indignant, and very frequently full of melancholy reflections upon that hard destiny which deprives him of the privileges of a free man, and obliges him to labour for an other"; moreover, slaves have opportunities to discuss plots of rebellion on such occasions. "Such a class of people your Petitioners would say are a Cancer on the breast of the body Politick and a Millstone hung around the necks of Masters." They therefore seek a law "to prohibit for the future the attendance of negro slaves at any Muster or Election ground."

Result: referred to committee; report unfavorable.

COMMENT: *It seems as though the petitioners knew well the evil depravation they forced upon the slaves and their yearnings of freedom.*

> "Is life so dear, or peace so sweet, as to be purchased at the price of chains and slavery? Forbid it, Almighty God! I know not what course others may take, but as for me, give me liberty or give me death. " –**Speech in the Virginia Convention 1775, Patrick Henry**.

***

Petition 11379303
South Carolina Charleston District/Parish
December 11, 1793

Abstract: "In behalf of the Whole," eight members of "The Society of Master Coopers of Charleston" express frustration at the "inattention" given by authorities to the law passed 10 May 1740 and revived 12 March 1783 regarding the management of slaves within the state. "[A]t present as well as for considerable Time past," they observe, "the Slaves of Charleston have been privileged (although illegally) to sell traffick and barter, as well as to carry on different Trades and Occupations (free from the Direction or Superintendence of any white Person whatever." They further declare that the black mechanics and tradesmen work "to their own Emolument and the great and manifest Injury of the mechanical part of the Community, selling their Commodities and working at their Trades much lower and at much cheaper Rates, than those persons who are privileged by their Citizenship." The petitioners believe such "Privileges encourage Negroes in Stealing as well as destroy that Subordination which the Situation of this State requires from the Slave towards his master and all other Citizens." The white coopers ask for an act of incorporation, with "Privileges and Rights as are usually granted in such Cases."

Result: referred to committee.

***

Petition 11685902
Virginia Louisa County
December 21, 1859
Abstract: Twenty-one residents of Prince George County insist that to protect the "due subordination of slaves to masters, & generally of the inferior black to the dominant white class," the assembly must address "two existing & wide-spread evils." These evils are 1) "the shops or other places for the unlicensed selling of intoxicating liquors to slaves" and the "carrying on with them other illegal traffic;" 2) "the intercourse with slaves, (& also with free negroes,) of persons, whether vagrants or temporary sojourners, who, in many cases, are either voluntary agents or hired emissaries of northern associations, or individuals, laboring to destroy slavery in the southern states, by instigating desertion, or conspiracy & insurrection." They seek new measures for the "prevention & punishment" of the twin evils.

Result: No recorded result.

***

Petition 11381608
South Carolina, Orangeburg District/Parish.
December 4, 1816
Abstract: Eleven citizens of Amelia Township, Orangeburg District, seek the passage of a law prohibiting slave owners from allowing their slaves to raise their own livestock or cotton. They argue that "every measure that may lessen the dependance of a slave on his master ought to be opposed, as tending to dangerous consequences. The more priviledges a slave obtains the less depending he is on his master & the greater nuisance he is likely to be to the public." They further insist that "of all their privileges that of their making cotton is the most objectionable." The petitioners purport that "Cotton is subject to the depredations of the night-walking thief and when lost it would be the height of folly to attempt to find it among negroes who all have

cotton of their own ... to authorise a slave to make cotton for himself is incouraging him to be a thief by putting him in the way of secreting what he steals." They declare that "a master may make what improvements he pleases in the lodging cloathing and food of his slave, in short there are many ways to encourage their industry without granting them privileges that would enable them to steal with impunity." The petitioners therefore pray "that it is highly necessary a law should be enacted this Session prohibiting negroes making cotton for themselves."

Result: referred to Judiciary Committee.

***

Petition 11381905
South Carolina Richland District/Parish
November 22, 1819
Abstract: Seventy-one white working men in Columbia seek legislation that prohibits slave owners from allowing skilled slaves to hire their own time. They suggest several "inconveniences & injuries arising from the aforesaid practice": that when slaves hire their time from their owners "to contract to do a job for any person, there is no remedy for his failing to do it"; a skilled slave, due to his "greater cheapness in his living ... is able to work cheaper & still make his wages than it is possible for white Journeymen to do & maintain their families"; and the wages of skilled slaves "in most cases" are "spent in the indulgence of vicious habits." The petitioners also request that "your Honourable Body see the necessity of prohibiting by Law such negro mechanics from taking apprentices to learn their respective Trades."

Result: referred to Judiciary Committee.

***

Petition 11382808
South Carolina, Charleston District/Parish

1828

Abstract: Joseph Johnson, Intendant of the Charleston City Council, raises many concerns to the members of the House of Representatives, one such concern being "the number of Schools publickly kept for the instruction of persons of Colour in reading and writing." Johnson is of the opinion that instruction is "injurious to the Community." He purports that "to be able to read and to write is certainly not necessary to the performance of those duties which are usually required of our Slaves and on the contrary is incompatible with the public safety." Johnson further argues that "the knowledge of the art of writing will enable persons of this class to carry on illicit traffic, to communicate privately among themselves and to evade those regulations that are intended to prevent confederations among them," whereby it will be "impossible to distinguish between the free and the slave of our coloured population." He therefore knows "of no remedy so effectual and at the same time so little liable to objection as the absolute prohibition of all Schools for the instruction of Coloured persons." In addition, Johnson asks that the practice of owners and others in hiring slaves and free persons of color in their stores and shops be halted. In addition to denying employment to the white population, this situation introduces "the Coloured population and especially slaves into situations which are inconsistent with their Condition." The petitioner suggests "that the system of slavery is so interwoven with the constitution of our Society that even if our interests permitted it would be impossible to eradicate it." He believes, therefore, that "it becomes highly important that the regulations necessary for maintaining this state of things in peace and security should be permanently established and regularly maintained."

Result: No recorded result.

Comments: Thank God for clear thinkers like Thomas Jefferson. In spite of his personal flaws, which we all have, his following comments were ahead of his time, and were prophetic in essence, and rang true for his posterity as an American.

> "I am not an advocate for frequent changes in laws and constitutions. But laws and institutions must go hand in hand with the progress of the human mind as that becomes more developed, more enlightened, as new discoveries are made new truths discovered and manners and opinions change, with the change of circumstances, institutions must advance also to keep pace with the times. We might as well require a man to wear still his coat which fitted him when a boy, as civilized society to remain ever under the regimen of their barbarous ancestors. I have sworn upon the alter of God eternal hostility against every form of tyranny over the mind of man. Freedom of religion; freedom of the press; freedom of person under the protection of habeas corpus."
> **-First inaugural address, Thomas Jefferson**.

***

Petition 11382813
South Carolina Charleston District/Parish
1828

Abstract: One hundred eleven "sundry mechanics of the City of Charleston" complain that they are suffering from a lack of trade and unemployment due to the unfair competition from "Negro and Colored Workmen." They suggest that the 1822 statute outlawing slave self-hire be amended "as to make it completely effective of its purpose." They lament "that almost all the Trades, but especially those of Carpenters, Bricklayers, Plasterers, Wheelwrights, House-painters, Shoe-makers, &c are beginning to be engrossed by Black & Colored workmen; that they are multiplying in a prodigious ratio; and, that Charleston, already swarming with a population of Free blacks, and of Slaves, more Licentious than if they were Free, must in a very short time be in the condition of a West Indian Town, which it will be impossible to defend without a Regular Military Force." They therefore pray "for such relief in the premises, as to your Honorable Body it may seem most expedient to grant them." The petitioners also request permission to form "themselves into an Association by the style of 'the Charleston Mechanics' Association'."

Result: No recorded result.

"When we go about our work earnestly and perseveringly, it often happens that   although we have to tack about again and again, we get ahead of those who are helped by the wind and tide." –Goethe.

***

Petition 11586101
Texas Harrison County
February 4, 1861

Abstract: Thirty-two white mechanics in Harrison County seek the passage of a bill "to prevent the competition and encouragement of Negro Mechanick." They believe that "it is not just or right to give Slaves the advantages or liberties that they are now endeavoring to take or get to put down white Workmen whose daily living is made by the sweat of their brow in their industrious pursuits." They "most solemnly object to being put in competition with Negro Mechanicks who are to rival us in the obtaining of contracts for the construction of Houses Churches and other Buildings." The petitioners declare "Negroes forever but Negroes in their places (viz: in Corn & Cotton Fields) and if there are those who have Negro Mechanicks to do their own work let them have them but we do not want to be equalized with them by allowing them to go at large contracting for jobs of work ... or to be made the Competitors of Negros in this a true Southern State." They ask that a law be passed "to confine them to the hire of some Workman or Undertaker whose duty it will be to keep them in their places and under proper control without the owner or Master being at all injured."

Result: referred to Committee on State Affairs.

Comments: The Negro Mechanics had tunnel-vision...for success...and they lived by tunneling... because they were a people buried alive beneath burdensome regulations and state-sponsored acts of oppression!

***

Petition 10382701
Delaware New Castle County
January 11, 1827
Abstract: The chairman of the Wilmington Union Colonization Society expresses concern about the expanding free black population. Robert Porter argues that free people of color do not and cannot enjoy the most important civil privileges (voting and office holding), cannot associate with whites, and will not be accepted on a basis of equality. Porter defends the legally sanctioned separation by declaring that "our separation from these people is the effect of moral causes, the foundations of which we could not safely remove; amalgamation would demoralize society; the consequence of breaking up the present distinctions would be not to raise the free coloured people, but to sink all to a state of degradation yet unknown." He therefore suggests "the removal of these people" to the west "coast of Africa" as the solution to what he describes "people by their very condition our enemies." In Porter's opinion, the American Colonization Society is deserving of more "of the resources of the National Government" and if the Society were able to make "this removal general and common, there can be no doubt, that this whole population would flow in a current in that direction."

Result: House: presented, read. Referred; Senate: read.

Comments: The free Black population lived in a social environment that was as cold as a record breaking winter's day...like those days that are so cold that as you moved from the unaffecting sunlight, to the shade as you scurried

about your business, you could feel the change in the
temperature run down your spine like water.

***

Petition 11379109
South Carolina Charleston District/Parish
January 1, 1791

Abstract: Charleston bricklayer Thomas Cole and butchers Peter Bassnett Mathewes and Matthew Webb represent that they "are deprived of the Rights and Privileges of Citizens" due to the act passed in 1740 "commonly called The Negroe Act." They state that they do not have "it in their power to give Testimony on Oath in prosecutions on behalf of the State"; they "are debarred of the Rights of Free Citizens of being subject to a Trial without the benefit of a Jury"; and they "are subject to Prosecution by Testimony of Slaves without Oath by which they are placed on the same footing." The petitioners report that "they have at all times since the Independence of the United States contributed and do now contribute to the support of Government by chearfully paying their Taxes." In addition, they "are ready and willing take and subscribe to such Oath of Allegiance to the States as shall be presented." While they "do not presume to hope that they shall be put on an equal footing with the Free White Citizens of this State," they do "humbly solicit such indulgence as the Wisdom and Humanity of this Honorable House shall dictate in their favor by repealing" the such clauses in the said Act that "will efectually Redress the grievances which your Memorialists humbly submit."

Result: rejected.

Comments: This group of petitions documents the calculated acts of legislation and public activism that denied the positive liberty of slaves; it denied them the right to be their own masters by manipulating their environment through politics and society, into a subculture. This is a powerful argument, even on the constitutional terms, because it asserts a conflict not just between liberty and equality but within society itself, because, the conflict between the enslaved and the free society could not be resolved simply because of the notion, that the "free" must be superior and sovereign. What should we make of the argument understood that way? Fortunately history has solved the problem for us and to avoid making those socially engineered mistakes again we must notice, first, that it remains a casual argument that every society and every people wants to be superior or sovereign. And that enslavement in America was a consequence or symptom of how the identity of a people had been reconstructed by a sovereign people, and an important cause or vehicle of that reconstruction was first to notice that the enslaved people were capable; equal in occupation; ideas and humanity...how else, could you control people if you did not know their potential?

***

Petition 20486237
District of Columbia Washington County
September 8, 1862
Abstract: On 16 April 1862, Congress passed an act abolishing slavery in the District of Columbia. Owners were required to file a schedule of slaves with the court, which issued certificates of freedom. On 12 July 1862, another act permitted minor or absentee owners and slaves themselves to file for certificates of freedom. Evelina Wedge, a "brown" female, between twenty-one and twenty-two years of age, who is the wife of a free man of color, George Wedge, states that she and her children, Martha A. E. Wedge and George Washington Wedge, are owned by Alexander McCormick. She seeks her freedom and the freedom of her children.

Result: No recorded result.

***

Petition 20486264
District of Columbia Washington County

July 22, 1862
Abstract: On 16 April 1862, Congress passed an act abolishing slavery in the District of Columbia. Owners were required to file a schedule of slaves with the court, which issued certificates of freedom. On 12 July 1862, another act permitted minor or absentee owners and slaves themselves to file for certificates of freedom. Mary Warrington, a "Light Mulatto" woman, twenty-five years of age, states that she is owned by Benjamin L. Jackson. She seeks her freedom.

Result: No recorded result.

Comments: A day, an hour of virtuous liberty, is worth a whole eternity of bondage.
–Addison's Cato.

***

The following extracts are compiled wants & warrants from "The suppressed book about slavery!" -**1864, by GEORGE W. CARLETON**.

Page: 296 DOMESTIC AMUSEMENTS IN THE SLAVE STATES.

" **Ran away** from the subscriber, living near Upper Marlboro', Prince George's county, Maryland, on Monday, the 28th August, a Negro boy, who calls himself Allen West. He is about 20 years of age, a bright light color, freckled face, straight red hair ; has a large scar on one of his wrists (caused by the bite of Mr. Pope's dog 'Taylor') ; he is about 5 feet 6 inches in height. He has relations living in Washington City. He has also a brother belonging to Richard B. B. Chew, Esq., and a sister belonging to Thomas Talbert, Esq. ; and his father belongs to Colonel William D. Bowie, and stays at his ' Bellfield plantation.' I have reason to believe he is endeavoring to pass himself off as a white boy! I will give $300 reward for his apprehension, if taken in a free State, or $100, if taken elsewhere, provided he is brought to me or secured in some jail so that I can get him. - **CHARLES CLAGETT.**

***

"$100 Reward."
The above reward will be paid for the apprehension of my Slave man William. He is of a very light color, and has straight yellowish hair. I have no doubt he will change his name, and try to pass himself for a white man, which he may be able to do, unless to a very close observer. - **T. S. PITCHAKD.**

***

Page: 300 DOMESTIC AMUSEMENTS IN THE SLAVE STATES.

Rappahannock Co., Va.
"Nov. 29."
Ran Away from the subscriber, living in the County of Rappahan- nock, on Tuesday last, Daniel, about 5 feet 8 inches high, about 35 years old, very intelligent, has been a wagoner for several years, and is pretty well acquainted from Richmond'to Alexandria. He calls himself Daniel Turner; his hair curls, without showing black blood, or wool; he has a scar on one cheek, and his left hand has been injured by a pistol-shot, and he
was shabbily dressed, when last seen. I will give $25 reward if taken out of the county, and secured in jail, so that I can get him, or $10, if taken in the county.- **A. M. WILLIS**.

***

Page: 301 DOMESTIC AMUSEMENTS IN THE SLAVE STATES.

Richmond (Va.) Whig
"$100 Reward will be given for the apprehension of my Negro, Edward Kenney. He has straight hair, and complexion so white that it is believed a stranger would suppose there was no African blood in him. He was with my

boy Dick a short time since in Norfolk, and offered him for Sale, and was apprehended, but escaped under pretence of being a
white man ! " - ANDERSON BOWLES.

***

Page: 340 DOMESTIC AMUSEMENTS IN THE SLAVE STATES.

" Greene County, Ala."
"Ran Away from the subscriber, working on the plantation of Col. II. Tinker, a boy, named Alfred. He is about eighteen years old, pretty well grown ; has blue eyes, light flaxen hair, and shin disposed to freckle. He will try to pass as freeborn. " - S. G. STEWART.

***

Page: 341 DOMESTIC AMUSEMENTS IN THE SLAVE STATES.

"Mobile, Ala."
"$10O Beward. — Ran away from the subscriber, a bright mulatto man-Slave, named Sam. Light, sandy hair, blue eyes, and ruddy com- plexion — is so white as very easily to pass for a free white man. -ED WIN PECK.

***

Page: 342 DOMESTIC AMUSEMENTS IN THE SLAVE STATES.

"Ran Away, or stolen, from the subscriber, living near Aberdeen,Miss., a light-colored Woman, of small size, and about 23 years of age. She has long, black, straight hair, and she usually keeps it in good order. When she left she had on

either a white dress, or a brown calico one Avith white spots or figures, and took with her a red handkerchief, and a red or pink sun-bonnet. She generally dresses very neatly. She calls her- self Mary Ann Paine — can read — has some freckles on her face and hands — Shoes No. 4 — had two rings on her fingers. She is very intel- ligent. Fifty dollars reward will be given for her, if taken out of the State, and twenty-five, if taken within the State.

***

Page: 343 DOMESTIC AMUSEMENTS IN THE SLAVE STATES.

New Orleans Picayune.

" **Ran Away** from the plantation of Madame Fergus Duplantier, on or about the 27th of June last, a boy named Ned ; he is stout-built, about five feet eleven inches high, and speaks English and French ; he is about thirty-five years of age. He may try to pass himself for a white man, as he is of a very clear color, and has sandy hair. Twenty-five dollars reward will be paid to whoever will bring him to Madame Duplanticr's plantation, Manchac, or lodge him in some jail, where he can be obtained."

***

New Orleans Delta.

"**Ran Away** from a Gang, in February last, a boy, named Nehemiah Adams. He is about five feet, three inches in height, with hazel eyes and brownish hair. He will not acknowledge that he is a Slave ; says his father is a white man and lives somewhere in Boston, Massachusetts. He is an habitual runaway, and was shot in the ankle while endeavoring to escape from Baton Rouge Jail. A reward of $325 will be paid on his delivery to me, or for his apprehension and commitment to any jail from which I can get him." - **A. L. BINGHAM.**

***

Page: 349 DOMESTIC AMUSEMENTS IN THE SLAVE STATES.

The Cincinnati (Ohio) Columbian, says, that a legal gentle-man of that City was called on in March, 1855, to write adeed of manumission to be given by a Louisiana planter to one of his Slaves, a young girl whom he had brought with him. As the description of the girl was somewhat curious, the Editor of The Columbian copied it from the deed : "Said Sarah Maria is 17 years of age, medium height, and rather slim figure, very fair complexion, with straight light brown hair, and hazel eyes, with features of the Caucasian race."

***

Chattanooga, Tenn
Date: approx 1855
" **$500 Reward**. — Ran away from the subscriber, on the 25th of May last, a Nigger boy, twenty-one years of age, named Washington. Said Nigger, without close observation, might pass himself for a white man, as he is light colored, has sandy hair, blue eyes, and a fine set of teeth. He is an excellent bricklayer; but I have no idea that he will pursue his trade, for fear of detection. Although he is like a white man in appearance, he has the disposition of a black Nigger," and delights in comic songs and witty expressions." He is an excellent house servant, very handy about a hotel ; tall and slender, and has rather a down look, especially when spoken to, and is sometimes inclined to be sulky. I have no doubt but he has been decoyed off by some Abolition scoundrel; and I will give the above reward for the apprehension of the boy and thief, if delivered at Chattanooga; or I will give $200 for the boy alone, or $100 if con- fined in any jail so that I cau get him.-The Chattanooga (Tenn) Gazette. - **GEORGE. 0. RAGLAND.**

***

Comments: *"The staple argument in favor of Slavery is based on the inferiority of the African blood, but as in more than half the States of the Republic three fourths or more of the blood is mixed with the blood of the "first families," such advertisements as the above are of every-day occurrence. Fathers advertise for, and hunt down with bloodhounds, their run-a- way Sons and Daughters, and Grandchildren, and catching them, sell them into Slavery." If a Slave can "pass himself off for white" he- is essentially white ; and the " Nigger argument" falls to the ground.* **-GEO W. CARLETON**.

***

A Nut from My Family Tree

It is probable that some of you reading this book may come across a petitions pertaining to one or more of your ancestors. If this occurs, I assure you, while it was my intention to publish these ancestral petitions; it is not my intention to embarrass the descendants. Demonstrating my sincerity I have included a very un-flattering court record about one of my ancestors.

It is apparent to me that some of my African Ancestors came to America as Slaves, and to my surprise I learned that some of my free White ancestors arrived here in chains as well, particularly Margaret Lawrence one of my Ancestral Grandmothers.

Having been indicted and convicted on a felony charge for theft in 1729, Margaret was expelled from England in bondage, banished to the colonies for 14 years, with 105 other prisoners, in March of 1730 aboard a sailing ship named the "Patapscoe Merchant".

In 1730, in colonial Maryland, she found herself on the auction block and spent the remainder of her life as an indentured servant in Virginia.

The following original text explains how Margaret Laurence, earned her ride to the US on the "Patapscoe Merchant":

The Proceedings of the Old Bailey
Ref: t17290827-32 ~ Original Text
August, 1729

- Margaret Laurence, of St. Andrew's Holborn, was indicted for that she, together with Esther Morgan, not taken, did feloniously steal a Gold Watch, Chain, and Seals, value 24 1. a Gold Snuff-Box, value 18 1. a Diamond Ear-ring, one Velvet Gown and Petticoat, and other Suits of silk Cloaths, and divers other wearing Apparel, Silk and Linen, as Head-Dress, Ruffles, Laces, &c. to the sum of 10 1. and 40 Guineas, the Goods of Martha Thorold, in the Dwelling-House of the said Martha Thorold, the 9th of July last.

- Madam Thorold depos'd, That the Prisoner had been her Servant, but had been gone from her about a Fortnight; and that she went out to pay a Visit about half an Hour after Five a-Clock in the afternoon, the 9th of July last, and returning Home about a half an Hour after Eight, could not get any Entrance; whereupon her Footman went round about, and got in the Back-way, where he found the Doors backwards all open, and opening the fore-Door, let her in, saying, Madam you are robb'd; that she going into her Rooms, found her Cabinet broken open, and the Drawers, &c. all thrown about the Room, and the Goods and Money mention'd in the indictment, gone, and finding her Servants, and examining them; Betty Loyd pretended to have been found, and that the Robbery was committed by two Persons, who they did believe were Men in Women's Cloths; and that the Servants did not own for a considerable time that they knew who the Persons were that had commited the Robbery.

- Elizabeth Loyd depos'd, That the Prisoner came about a Fortnight after she had left Madam Thorold's Service, along with Hester Morgan, to their House; that they ask'd them to stay all Night, which they did, and all the next Day, 'till her Mistress were gone out; after which, Margaret Laurence pull'd her into th Men's Room, telling her, She had her Mistress and thrown her down on the Bed, took off her Garters, and tied her Hands, &c. with her Garters, and then went and rifled the House; that they were busy in doing it for about 3 quarters of an Hour, and afterwards she say the go out at the Back-Door, having each of them a large Bundle under their Riding-Hoods; but she could not tell what was in them.

- Lucy Hart depos'd, That She being busy in getting up Mrs. Thorold's Head-cloaths, heard Betty Loyd shriek out, and presently the Prisoner and Hester Morgan came into the Room, and told her, They had a mind to rob Mrs. Thorold of her Money; that she desir'd them not to talk of any such thing; her Conscience would not let her consent to it; the the Prisoner replied, If Taylor and Weldon (two former Servants) had been there, they would have been glad of the Opportunity; that she not consenting, but crying out, Hester Morgan damn'd her, and threatened her, that if she made any Noise of Opposition, she would kill her; that they at first ty'd her, but afterwards let her loose again, and lock'd her up.

- Thomas Booth, the Constable, depos'd, That the Prisoner being apprehended, did at last own the Fact; that she had pawn'd a Pair of Stays a Gown and Petticoat of Mrs. Thorolds, and told them where Hester Morgan lodged, at one Forster's, a Shoemaker in Tash-Street; that he went thither, and Hester Morgan being gone out, he demanded the Key; but that not being deliver'd, he search'd the Room, but not finding them; after menacing the People of the House, was told, that the Goods had been carried to a Trunkmaker's in Holborn, which by Enquiry being found, they were inform'd that Morgan having bought a large Trunk the Things were put into it, and carried away by a Porter; the the Porter being found, he carried him to one Mr. Busby's, where it was found; but Hester Morgan was not there, not had they yet had an Opportunity of apprehending her.

- Mr. Busby depos'd, That she had known Hester Morgan several Years, and took her for an honest Person; that meeting with her, she said she was coming out of Place, and desir'd her to recommend her to a Lodging in an honest House, whereupon she told her she might lodge with her, and the Trunk and a Bundle was brought in: The Constable added, That the Prisoner being ask'd the reason whe she had robb'd Madam Thorold? she replied, That she did it not for Want, but for Spite, she having us'd her ill.

- Mr. Chambers, the Pawn-broker, depos'd, That having heard of Madam Thorold's being robb'd, and suspecting that the Stays, Gowns, &c. which the Prisoner had pawn'd to him, were Madam Thorold's, he went and acquainted her he had such Things, which she having own'd, they were produced in Court, own'd by the Prosecutor, and sworn to be pawn'd by the Prisoner.

- The Prisoner in her Defence pleaded, that she receiv'd those Cloaths from Hester Morgan, to pawn for her, who pretended that Madam Thorold had given them to her. She pleaded likewise, that Elizabeth Loyd desir'd her to take off her Garters, and bind her with them and likewise to Gag her, that her Mistress might have no Suspicion of her; that the Evidences, Loyd, Hart, and Morgan, had contriv'd the Robbery, and she had been sent to for Several times to commit it, and that they were all four to have gone down into Wales; and that she had note of the Things but the Gown, Petticoat and Stays before-mention'd, and knew but of 12 Guineas to have been taken by Morgan. The Fact being plainly prov'd, the Jury found her guilty of the Indictment. Death.

- At receiving Sentence, the Prisoner did not, as usual, plead her Belly, but begg'd of the Court to consider that she was a young Person, and threw herself upon the Mercy of the Court.

- Esther Morgan. . . . . On October 15, 1729 Esther Morgan was charged in Court with the same charges as Margaret, with the same result, Guilty of the Indictment. Death.

***

In closing, if we assume that the importance of these legal documents lies in the fact that they gives us an understanding of the state of mind and economics of our ancestors in their respective epochs, would mean these are merely historical documents. I would rather think the association fosters an aesthetic and spiritual connection between us and our ancestors. This is explained by the fact that in their societies, in spite of their color differences, they shared certain common traits that developed into customs and courtesies that affects us today. Indeed today we are still trying to shake off stereotypes and myths that were harmful then and are harmful now... and hold onto broad, intense and powerful Associations that were pleasurable then and are pleasurable now.

The readings of these petitions, citations, exhortations and expressions have raised them above and beyond the limitation of being merely representations of the society of those days.

> "The heritage of the past is the seed that brings forth the harvest of the future." -**Archives Building, Washington, DC.**

www.ingramcontent.com/pod-product-compliance
Lightning Source LLC
Chambersburg PA
CBHW051506170526
45166CB00001B/408